Mentoring young people leaving care

'Someone for me'

Jasmine Clayden and Mike Stein

JOSEPH ROWNTREE
FOUNDATION

The **Joseph Rowntree Foundation** has supported this project as part of its programme of research and innovative development projects, which it hopes will be of value to policy makers, practitioners and service users. The facts presented and views expressed in this report are, however, those of the authors and not necessarily those of the Foundation.

Joseph Rowntree Foundation
The Homestead
40 Water End
York YO30 6WP
Website: www.jrf.org.uk

Mike Stein is a research professor in the Social Work Research and Development Unit at the University of York. For the past 25 years he has been researching the problems and challenges faced by young people leaving care. He has published extensively in this field and was involved in the preparation of the Guidance for the Children (Leaving Care) Act 2000.

Jasmine Clayden is a research fellow in the Social Work Research and Development Unit at the University of York. She has been involved in research into young people leaving care, young people running away from care, family support teams and mentoring for care leavers.

ISBN 1 85935 401 7   (paperback)
ISBN 1 85935 402 5   (pdf: available at www.jrf.org.uk)

A CIP catalogue record for this report is available from the British Library.

Cover design by Adkins Design

Prepared and printed by:
York Publishing Services Ltd
64 Hallfield Road
Layerthorpe
York YO31 7ZQ
Tel: 01904 430033;   Fax: 01904 430868;   Website: www.yps-publishing.co.uk

Further copies of this report, or any other JRF publication, can be obtained either from the JRF website (www.jrf.org.uk/bookshop/) or from our distributor, York Publishing Services Ltd, at the above address.

Contents

Acknowledgements

We wish to acknowledge the help we received from James Cathcart and the Prince's Trust in accessing the mentoring projects that participated in the original research. We were also greatly helped by the project leaders who we interviewed and who assisted us in the collection of data, as well as the setting up of interviews with mentors and young people.

We also valued the contributions made to this study by the members of the Advisory Group: David Berridge, Mark Burrows, James Cathcart, Joyce Harvey, Janet Lewis Jones, Maggie Jones, Charlie Lloyd, Leonie Paul and Maxine Wrigley. We are grateful to JRF, which funded the project, and Charlie Lloyd, our JRF research adviser, who has been very helpful and constructive throughout the research process.

Finally, we wish to thank the young people and their mentors for sharing their experiences with us. We hope that we have captured the essence of their mentoring relationships in this report.

1 Mentoring care leavers

Mentors are everywhere these days. They are to be found in schools, colleges, places of work, as well as in a variety of projects assisting young people who are variously labelled 'antisocial', 'disadvantaged', 'disaffected', 'socially excluded' or 'vulnerable'. The 'Big Idea' of mentoring originated from the United States where the early 'Big Brother, Big Sister' projects were pioneered and where belief in mentoring interventions has continued to fuel their expansion. In part influenced by these developments, mentoring has become a significant component of contemporary government youth policy in the United Kingdom, even though it has been subject to little conceptual interrogation or research into its effectiveness.

What is mentoring?

In the literature, mentoring is used to describe many different types of relationships – there is no simple definition or classification. However, different forms of mentoring have been defined by:

- their *origin*, whether 'naturally' occurring within families or communities as distinct from 'artificial' or professionally promoted

- the *type of mentoring relationship* : one-to-one; one-to-group; peer mentoring

- the *site of mentoring*, for example, whether the mentoring takes place in a school, workplace, project or local community setting.

Beyond these descriptive dimensions, studies have suggested different models or approaches to mentoring that are pertinent to our present study.

First of all, the *purpose* of mentoring schemes can be defined on a continuum. This may begin with 'instrumental' or 'engagement mentoring' linked to 'hard' outcomes, such as employment, education or training, or reducing offending behaviour, and continue to more 'expressive' mentoring linked to 'soft' outcomes, such as self-esteem and personal development.

Second, the *process* of mentoring can be located on a 'service-led' to 'participatory' continuum, identifying the extent to which goals are defined by the mentoring service (or project) or are initiated by, negotiated with and agreed by the mentored young person.

Does mentoring work?

Two research reviews of the impact of mentoring schemes carried out in the United States suggest we should be cautious about making major claims for their efficacy. The first review, published in 1997, drew attention to the lack of controlled evaluations as a basis to guide policy – there simply wasn't the research evidence at that time (Sherman *et al.*, 1997). A second, later, review (DuBois *et al.*, 2002), derived from a meta-analysis of 55 evaluations, concluded that mentoring schemes can have an impact on outcomes. The evidence was strongest for problem behaviours, and education and employment outcomes, and less certain for social, emotional and psychological adjustment. However, the researchers' analysis showed that the effect on all these areas was very small.

There have been very few controlled evaluations of mentoring carried out in the United Kingdom. The only recent outcomes study using a participating cohort and a comparison sample – an evaluation of Mentoring Plus for disaffected young people – assessed the impact of the programme in relation to engagement with education, training and work, family relationships, offending, substance use and self-esteem. It found that the programme had an impact on education, training and work, but not on any of the other areas (Shiner *et al.*, 2004).

The same study, in response to over-simplified, goal-orientated 'progression models', captured the process of mentoring as three potential cycles. First, the basic cycle: 'mundane' contact–meeting–doing. Second, the problem-solving cycle: contact–meeting–doing–fire-fighting, and, third, the action-orientated cycle: contact–meeting–doing–fire-fighting–action. The researchers suggested that, for most young people:

> … mentoring is a delicate process based on ordinary social interaction … typically it is cyclical and reactive.
> (Shiner *et al.*, 2004, *Findings*, p.2)

There have, however, been a number of descriptive studies. Listening to the views of young people and mentors, through mainly small-scale qualitative studies, adds a different dimension. A recent study looked at the impact of mentoring on young people who were described as 'socially excluded, vulnerable or disaffected' in three settings (Philip *et al.*, 2004). Two of the projects used paid key workers as mentors and the third, a befriending scheme, used volunteer mentors. The study found that mentoring offered a kind of 'professional friendship' where both parties negotiated what they would discuss and the time they would give to the relationship.

Young people found the mentoring experience to be generally positive. It contributed to developing their confidence and skills and helped them in other ways, for example, coming to terms with difficult family situations. The young people particularly appreciated mentors who shared a similar background and experience to themselves and were willing to talk about it.

Mentors also found the relationship satisfying as they were working *with* rather than *on* the young people. However, while volunteer mentors highlighted the social nature of their role, the paid key workers were more concerned with changing the young people's behaviour in some way.

The study also found that the process of ending a relationship was a key element in looking at its success. If the ending was not handled sensitively it could undo the benefits of the relationship. Young people also valued the relationship continuing on an, albeit informal, basis after its official ending.

The study concluded that mentoring must be part of a range of support available for vulnerable young people. Some mentoring approaches suited the individual needs of young people better than others and the authors suggest there needs to be a variety of mentoring projects available (Philip *et al.*, 2004).

Recent accounts of mentoring have been criticised for their failure to acknowledge the context in which mentoring takes place, in particular their disregard for social and economic policies and structures, as well as the power relations that may pervade mentoring relationships (Colley, 2003). Research carried out by the same author has also shown how a rigid adherence to instrumental goals may undermine expressive achievements (Colley, 2003).

Mentoring for care leavers

The policy context

Mentoring for care leavers is a relatively recent development in the United Kingdom. During 1998, the Prince's Trust and Camelot Foundation set up the first network of locally based mentoring projects for care leavers, in partnership with the National Children's Bureau. In this context, mentoring was seen as providing additional support to a group of highly vulnerably young people during their transition to independence, a transition that research had shown was more accelerated, more compressed and less supported than for many of their peers (Stein, 2004).

The findings from research studies in the different UK jurisdictions contributed to an increased awareness of the problems faced by care leavers including the limitations of discretionary child welfare and social policy legislation, and the wide variations between areas in the level and quality of leaving care services (see Stein, 2004 for a review of the research).

The newly elected 1997 Labour Government, in its response to the Children's Safeguards Review – following the revelations of widespread abuse in children's homes – committed itself to legislate for new and stronger duties in relation to care leavers. Sir William Utting, who chaired the Review, had drawn attention to the plight of 16-year-old care leavers:

> ... unsupported financially and emotionally, without hope of succour in distress.
> (Utting, 1997)

The proposed changes, detailed in the consultation document, *Me, Survive, Out There?* (Department of Health, 1999), were to build on Labour's modernisation programme for children's services in England. This included the Quality Protects initiative introduced in England in 1998, providing substantial central government funding linked to specific service objectives. In relation to young people leaving care, objective 5 was to:

> ... ensure that young people leaving care, as they enter adulthood, are not isolated and participate socially and economically as citizens.
> (Department of Health, 1998)

Three performance indicators linked to this objective were:

> ... for young people looked after at the age of 16, to maximise the number engaged in education, training or employment at 19; to maximise the number of young people leaving care after their sixteenth birthday who are still in touch ... on their nineteenth birthday; to maximise the number of young people leaving care on or after their sixteenth birthday who have suitable accommodation at the age of 19.
> (Department of Health, 1998)

Also, in England, wider government initiatives to combat social exclusion, including the introduction of the Connexions Service and initiatives to tackle youth homelessness, under-achievement in education, employment and training, and teenage parenthood, are intended to impact on care leavers (Social Exclusion Unit, 1998a, 1998b, 1999).

Against this background, the Children (Leaving Care) Act 2000 was introduced in England and Wales in October 2001. Its main aims are to delay young people's transitions from care until they are prepared and ready to leave; strengthen the assessment, preparation and planning for leaving care; provide better personal support for young people after care; and improve the financial arrangements for care leavers.

To meet these aims, the provisions of the Act apply to different groups of 'eligible', 'relevant', 'former relevant' and 'qualifying' young people – see Chapter 2 of the Guidance for a clear explanation of who gets what (Department of Health, 2001). The key responsibilities are:

- to assess and meet the needs of young people in and leaving care

- pathway planning

- the appointment of a personal adviser to provide advice and support to young people, to participate in needs assessment and pathway planning, to co-ordinate services, to be informed about progress and well-being, and to keep records of contact

- assistance with education and training up to the age of 24

- financial support and maintenance in suitable accommodation

- for the 'responsible authority' to keep in touch, that is the local authority that 'looked after' the young person.

The research context

It was against this policy background that the Prince's Trust mentoring projects were operating. They had two main objectives. First, to offer young people aged 16–21 leaving care the support of their own volunteer mentor. Second, to introduce care leavers to a range of opportunities through the Prince's Trust grants and programmes. The present authors were previously commissioned by the Prince's Trust to carry out a descriptive evaluation of their work 2000–02 (Clayden and Stein, 2002). The main findings from this earlier study included the following.

- The Prince's Trust network of mentoring project work with severely disadvantaged young people leaving care: many of these young people were disadvantaged in terms of their education with high rates of school exclusion or suspension and subsequent low levels of attainment. Many were, or had been, involved in substance abuse or in trouble with the police. Homelessness and running away were often features of their lives. Some were isolated and out of touch with their birth families.

■ Nearly two-thirds of the young people surveyed were still involved in mentoring relationships between six and 12 months after they had started being mentored. They made contact with their mentors through face-to-face meetings, as well as a variety of other forms of communication, including telephone, text messaging, email and letter.

■ Mentors and young people both reported working on the areas of self-confidence and self-esteem. Young people reported that mentors had helped them in these areas by 'being there' for them, listening to them and challenging them.

■ Mentors helped young people to achieve their personal goals and often young people achieved goals not specified at the start of their mentoring relationship.

■ Mentors helped to raise the aspirations of the young people they were working with by providing them with appropriate role models. For this to work successfully, careful matching of mentors and mentees needed to take place.

■ Mentors offered a range of support to young people through the mentoring process. They offered practical support in the young people's transitions to independence in terms of support, help and advice concerned with housing issues, education and employment. They also offered emotional support to the young people by spending specific time with them and listening to them.

■ This research found no relationship between age, gender or ethnic origin in terms of how likely a mentoring relationship was to be successful. Success was more likely to be dependent on careful matching of mentors and young people, and flexible approaches of project managers, within safe guidelines.

The research described above was concerned with the outcomes at the end of the mentoring relationships, after six to 12 months. But we knew very little about longer-term mentoring relationships or outcomes.

The current study

The current study was carried out over a two-year period (2002–04).

The young people included in the research started being mentored between 1 March 2000 and 28 February 2002. They consisted of young people who had been in mentoring relationships lasting between six months and three years (longer-term mentoring) and also those who had been mentored for less than six months whose mentoring relationships had ended two to fours years prior to our study (mentoring longer term).

The current study was able to select 20 projects that participated in our Prince's Trust evaluation and were continuing to offer a mentoring service for care leavers. Selection was based on a number of factors, including the anticipated availability and number of potential research respondents and the willingness of the co-ordinator to participate in the research. All projects in the research frame were visited to explain the research in more detail and discuss details of their involvement, as well as to explore the feasibility of doing a case file study in each of the projects.

The study was based on quantitative data derived from a file search (database analysis) and qualitative information from interviews with young people, their mentors and project co-ordinators.

The database sample: file search

Having started with 20 projects, it was possible to carry out a file search in only 14 projects (two of the co-ordinators chose not to continue to take part in the research, three co-ordinators felt that they would be unable to trace any of the young people mentored during the research period, four of the co-ordinators had left or were due to leave shortly and a fire had destroyed the files in one project).

The initial file search carried out at the projects included all young people who started being mentored between 1 March 2000 and 28 February 2001. This was then extended to include young people who began being mentored to 28 February 2002 in order to maximise the potential sampling frame.

Case file studies enabled data to be gathered on the following areas:

■ profile of young people – age, gender, ethnic origin

- profile of their mentors – age, gender, ethnic origin

- data on the matching process, including time between referral and matching, and whether young people had a choice of mentor

- reasons for referring a young person to a mentoring project and reasons why young people wanted mentors

- objectives and goals of the mentoring process

- activities undertaken by mentors and mentees as part of the mentoring process

- outcomes data, including goals achieved.

Outcome measures were compiled from a combination of recording sheets of mentoring sessions completed by mentors, notes written by project co-ordinators and records of final interviews with young people. In the main, there was thus a qualitative measure of outcomes and goals achieved. Included in these outcome measures were both 'hard' outcomes (for example, progress with education, gaining employment) and 'soft' outcomes (for example, improving and maintaining relationships, gaining self-confidence or self-esteem).

In order to make a judgement on whether outcomes were positive or negative for each young person, a rigorous research methodology was adopted. For an outcome to be judged either positive or negative, evidence had to be gleaned from the young person's file, whether this be through mentor reports of mentoring sessions, records of meetings between the co-ordinator and the young person, or quarterly summary sheets written by the co-ordinator.

There were limitations to the data, as it was collated from project files that were kept as administrative records of mentors, young people and some of the activities they engaged in. The information collected was not always uniform, as projects answered to different organisations that had different information needs and priorities. Also, a large part of the data has been drawn from recording sheets of mentoring sessions completed by mentors, although not all the mentors completed these rigorously or even regularly. In the peer-mentoring project, young people had requested that this sort of record was not kept and so in that case data was collected verbally from the project co-ordinator, based on their personal knowledge and experience of working with the young people. The data gathered was collated in a systematic way using a preconstructed database to reduce the amount of bias that may have been created by incomplete data.

The interview sample

The sampling frame for the interviews consisted of all young people who began being mentored between 1 March 2000 and 28 February 2002 in the selected projects. A decision was taken to concentrate on fewer of the projects and to maximise the sample within those rather than select the interview sample from all of the projects taking part in the research. However, the response rate was poor because of a combination of the following factors:

■ high rate of geographical mobility among care leavers

■ some of the young people now in their early twenties had moved on in their lives and did not want to take part in the research

■ lack of 'follow-up' policies (beyond the original remit of 12 months)

■ staff turnover among project co-ordinators (who often knew the young people very well)

■ varying quality of record-keeping within many projects.

A total of 148 young people from 11 projects were written to inviting them to take part in the research. This represented all of the young people who started being mentored in the research 'window'. We were hoping to recruit a larger sample – about 20 per cent of these young people (29). In the event, despite considerable efforts, 17 young people were interviewed. We recognise that these 17 may not have been representative of all mentored young people, as they still had some contact with the mentoring projects and were thus geographically stable. Data was collected on:

■ young people's education, training and employment, accommodation, hobbies and interests, and professional support at the time they started being mentored and subsequently

■ young people's mentoring experience and support from their mentor

■ where mentors were unable to help

■ young people's views of outcomes; achievement while being mentored; accommodation; education, employment and training; relationships; hobbies and interests; problem areas; self-esteem and confidence

- young people's perception of the impact of mentoring on their lives

- reflections on the mentoring process

- young people's future plans.

Interviews were also carried out with mentors of 12 of the young people to gather data on:

- mentor profile; motivation for mentoring; previous experience of working with young people; mentor training; mentor support; matching

- the mentoring relationship; the intensity of the relationship; the nature of the relationship; planning and goal setting

- mentor's perception of the impact of mentoring on specified outcome areas and mentoring 'making a difference'

- the impact of mentoring on the mentor, reflecting on the mentoring relationship.

Finally, detailed interviews were carried out with ten project co-ordinators or managers covering the following:

- the need for the mentoring project, resources and staffing, funding issues

- project design, purpose and focus

- project growth and development

- mentor selection, matching, training and support

- problem areas/issues, including boundaries

- length of relationships and mentor commitment

- feedback obtained from young people and mentors about their mentoring experiences.

The names of the young people, their mentors and the projects have been changed to protect their anonymity.

Outline of the report

Chapter 2 describes the main activities of the mentoring projects that participated in the research (see also the Appendix). In Chapter 3, we present the findings from our analyses of 181 longer-term mentoring relationships from 13 of these projects. This is organised around the profile of the young people, referral, plans and goals, mentor activity, outcomes and mentor profiles. Findings from our interviews with our young people and their mentors are presented in Chapter 4. Chapter 5 describes how mentors saw their role and includes their views of, and motivation for, mentoring, as well as how they saw the training and support they were offered. What has been the impact of mentoring in the lives of the young people? It is this question that is explored in Chapter 6. This will include an exploration of how young people and their mentors thought mentoring made a difference to their lives, the longer-term impact of being mentored, as well as the impact of mentoring on the mentors. In Chapter 7, we conclude by summarising our findings.

2 The mentoring projects

> What do we aim to do? … Reduce loneliness and anxiety, develop skills
> and confidence and help young people fulfil their potential.
> (Project co-ordinator)

The mentoring relationships we were interested in originated in the mentoring
projects.[1] This chapter is based on interviews with project co-ordinators from ten of
the mentoring projects set up under the Prince's Trust Leaving Care Initiative. It
begins with a profile of the projects and explores why the projects were set up, their
programme structure, and their funding and staffing. This is followed by a discussion
of the projects' aims and activities relating to the mentoring process.

Profile of the projects

The projects began between 1998 and 2000 being initiated and funded by the
Prince's Trust Leaving Care Initiative, although one project was set up in 1995 but
gained Prince's Trust funding in 1999. The Prince's Trust laid down a set of minimum
standards that the projects had to meet and sign up to, in order to gain funding from
them (Cathcart, 2003).

The definition of mentoring on which the Prince's Trust model was based was that
suggested by the Home Office:

> Mentoring is a one-to-one, non-judgemental relationship in which an
> individual mentor voluntarily gives time to support and encourage
> another. This is typically developed at a time of transition in the mentee's
> life, and lasts for a significant and sustained period of time.
> (Active Community Unit, Home Office, www.mandbf.org.uk/
> mentoring_and_befriending/25)

An examination of the mission statements of the projects shows that the aims of
these ten projects were not primarily to change young people's behaviour but to offer
them support during their transition to independence, including helping them to
develop their skills. A detailed description of the work of the projects is presented in
the Appendix.

Why the need for mentoring projects?

While the impetus for some of the social services departments to set up mentoring projects seems to have been an approach by the Prince's Trust, others had identified a gap in their provision of services to care leavers. Two of the social services departments had been involved in research where the young people identified feelings of isolation and a lack of support during their transition to independence.

The voluntary organisation behind one of the projects recognised that care leavers had a high incidence of mental health problems and felt that a mentoring project would provide an invaluable service to these young people. This led it to approach social services in order to help provide this service. At the same time, the social services department was aware that it was not offering care leavers as much support as they needed.

For all the projects involved in the research, mentoring was clearly seen as an extra service to be available to the young people rather than replacing any service they were currently receiving under the Children (Leaving Care) Act 2000.

Programme structure

All of the projects initially adopted a one-to-one mentoring model for young people leaving care at least from age 16 to 21, and two of these projects encompassed peer mentoring in their design. Peer mentors were slightly older care leavers who would guide their young people through the complex process of leaving care and moving to independent living by drawing on their own experiences. The model adopted was that laid down in the Prince's Trust minimum standards.

The co-ordinators variously describe the relationships in the initial design from befriending to task-focused relationships, that is, the expressive–instrumental dimensions or continuum described in Chapter 1. At the stage when the projects were set up, mentors were expected to work with young people to produce action plans in the relationships, but this focus changed as the projects developed. Action plans were agreed goals that the young person wanted to work towards with the support of their mentor.

Five of the projects based the design of their programme on the National Children's Bureau model that was developed as part of the Prince's Trust Leaving Care Initiative and included a minimum of 20 hours' training and ongoing support of mentors, and the others followed the general Prince's Trust standards.

Overall, our interviews with project leaders suggest that there is no uniform development of mentoring relationships in these projects. One project co-ordinator felt that relationships developed from a befriending role, and it was only when trust had been built up between the mentor and young person that goals emerged. Another project co-ordinator believed that the relationships developed by being task-focused initially but then matured to one where they were able to offer emotional support to the young person:

> I think they begin with that [goals] and then frequently what happens is the young person really just wants to have someone to talk to ... so some will almost turn into just a lot of emotional support, which I think is probably more important than focusing on how to cook a lasagne.
> (City 3)

The projects all consulted young people before they were matched with a mentor to find out their views and expectations of mentoring.

Peer mentoring

Two of the projects were already involved in peer mentoring and for one of these it was its main focus. In these projects, young people who had already passed through the care system and had made the transition to independent living were trained as mentors for young people still to complete this transition. The peer-mentoring project also offered young people an adult mentor where this was considered more appropriate – the few young people who wanted this were referred to a different agency for this type of mentoring.

This project also caters for many 'unaccompanied asylum-seeking and refugee young people', the number and proportion of whom are increasing. The local authority sees peer mentoring and group work as particularly suitable for helping these young people. Only about one-third of referred young people are British born and the project has positively discriminated to include these young people, as it is harder to get them involved and their outcomes have tended to be poorer than the other project users.

Links with aftercare teams

Four of the projects were based within local authority aftercare teams, although one of these had only just been located with the team and a further project was due to share office space on a reciprocal agreement. For the other projects, it had taken considerable time to build up relationships with the aftercare team to the extent that they recognised the value and contribution of the mentoring project and were prepared to make referrals to them.

Another project, managed by a voluntary organisation, was having difficulties getting the social services aftercare team to recognise the project, as there was some confusion about whether it was appropriate to refer young people to a project not funded by them. However, this was resolved once they understood how the Prince's Trust funding worked.

Funding, resources and staffing

Only a minority of the project co-ordinators felt that the level of resources they were working with was adequate. The main issues identified by the project leaders included: lack of administrative support; split responsibilities for project leaders – between mentoring and other leaving care work; lack of preparation for their mentoring co-ordinator's role – having to shape own role; and insecure and short-term funding – having to raise funds and prepare funding bids.

Other activities

Many of the projects were not involved solely in providing a mentoring service for care leavers and this was particularly the case where co-ordinators did not work full time on supporting mentoring. Some of the co-ordinators were responsible for managing other projects, for example, a mentoring project for young parents, mentoring for young offenders, a drop-in for care leavers and a job club.

Other project co-ordinators were involved in training independent visitors, training for foster carers, co-ordinating the production of a magazine by and for care leavers, supervising social work students, lecturing, training for providers of supported lodgings and employers who take on care leavers. One co-ordinator organised art workshops and celebration events for young people, as well as managing a peer-mentoring project to meet the health and mental health needs of young people. Project co-ordinators were also involved in fundraising on behalf of the mentoring projects.

What the projects do – project focus

The main aim of the projects was focused around the service they offered to young people, including the selection and recruitment of mentors:

> … to help young people develop their individual skills, knowledge and abilities to successfully make the transition from public care to independent living. To generally assist young people in their growth as individuals.
> (Borough 4)

> ... to recruit and train members of the local community to befriend and provide ongoing assistance to vulnerable young people who have moved to independence from the 'looked-after' system.
> (Borough 3 and City 4)

The co-ordinators of the projects located with local leaving care teams often knew the young people before they were referred to the team. Where this was not the case, co-ordinators made a point of meeting with and talking to the young people about why they wanted a mentor and what sort of things they wanted to do with them.

Of those volunteering to be mentors, not all proceed through the training and become matched with young people. They can be deselected because of difficulties like severe mental health problems, the desire to 'social work' young people rather than be a mentor to them, or perhaps because they have been in care themselves and are still very angry and in need of resolution work. Other reasons given were because the volunteer was too quiet or non-participative, too overbearing or homophobic, etc.

Mentor selection

The procedure for mentor selection was similar across the projects. On receipt of an enquiry, potential mentors are sent an information pack and application form. After submitting their application, in some projects they are called for individual interview, in others to a group selection day. If they are still considered suitable, they are then offered a place on the next available training course. At this stage a Criminal Records Bureau check is done and references taken up. Mentors are continually assessed throughout the training and, at the end of the course, there is usually another one-to-one interview.

Several of the co-ordinators commented that they were unable to meet the demand for mentors from the young people. One co-ordinator received an average of 22 referrals a month but had the resources to train only 20 mentors a quarter! In most of the projects, young people were involved in some way with mentor selection. They either sat on the individual interview panels or were involved in the group selection days.

Training

All of the projects reported that they had increased the amount of training offered to mentors. The basic training course was also longer now, between 30 and 50 hours for most of the projects, whereas most had begun by offering a 24-hour training course, as this was the minimum standard laid down by the Prince's Trust. In addition to the basic training, the projects offered either ongoing training or sessions on more specialised topics, e.g. substance abuse, Indian head massage. Some projects also referred mentors for other training available in the community, e.g. first aid, writing skills. The projects ran between one and four training courses a year and, for most, this was subject to demand, resources and/or the need to meet training targets. Two of the project co-ordinators felt that lack of resources hampered their ability to meet the demand for trained mentors.

As mentioned above, not all volunteers go on to become mentors. Between 50 and 95 per cent succeeded in completing the training and selection programme. However, for these, there could still be a wait before being matched with a young person. The peer-mentoring project also used the training as a kind of development programme for the young people. About half of these were not likely to become mentors for a long time because they did not have either the necessary skills or the confidence, but it was felt that they would benefit from the training process anyway.

These young people were often involved in running group work in the project or helping with the organisation. About eight of the young people trained as exit interviewers talking to young people in or leaving care about placement moves.

Young people were involved in both the training and interviews in the Borough 4 project, as the co-ordinator felt that this helped to break down stereotypes about young people who had been in care.

Support of mentors

All of the mentors were offered both individual supervision and group supervision in all of the projects, although not necessarily on a regular basis. Group supervision was generally organised on a monthly, six-weekly or quarterly basis. Whereas some co-ordinators reported that these sessions were well attended by mentors, others found them to be only sporadically attended. Group supervision was also used by some of the projects to deliver additional training sessions. One of the projects used the opportunities afforded by their drop-in to do group supervision and thus it was slightly more informal and ad hoc in nature.

Individual supervision also took place in all of the projects. Again the frequency varied across the projects from monthly to quarterly. At the peer-mentoring project, the individual supervision sessions were more ad hoc and the co-ordinator was in constant contact with the mentors and the young people mainly through the group work. In addition, if the mentor had major concerns about their mentee, they were able to contact the social worker direct, as well as the co-ordinator. In Borough 4, the individual supervision was held at the behest of the mentors rather than on a regular basis. However, the co-ordinator monitored the contact and would telephone the mentor if they had not been in touch for a while.

All of the co-ordinators were available by telephone to their mentors should any problems or queries arise. This was often by mobile phone, which mentors could contact out of hours. Two of the projects were using email to keep in touch with their mentors. One of the co-ordinators used this as a form of supervision and feedback with their mentors.

In one of the projects, the mentors had set up their own informal group for discussion, as well as exchanging telephone numbers so that they could offer each other support; while, in another project, near a city centre, mentors frequently called in at the office if they were nearby. At this project, one-to-one supervision was held only at key times in the relationship, although newer mentors were offered more support. This accessibility was therefore very valuable for these mentors. 'Resting' mentors were sent a newsletter to keep them in touch with the project and were encouraged to take part in the drop-in or get involved with other related projects across the city.

Matching

Matching was a key process in creating successful mentoring relationships. One of the co-ordinators in particular carried this out in quite an analytical way, considering things like personality traits, position in family, maternity and similar physical characteristics. This method was not always successful, although the co-ordinator did think it worked in most cases. She also knew both the young person and mentor prior to matching. In other projects, both mentors and mentees completed matching forms that identified areas, such as skills, interests, distances they could travel and how much time they had available.

Young people were usually also asked why they wanted a mentor and what type of mentor they would prefer, although this was not always the case. They may then be asked why they had made these particular preferences. In all the projects, young people could terminate a relationship at any time if they were not happy about the match. In most of these cases, both mentor and young person would be eligible for rematching. In one of the projects, the young people did not complete forms prior to matching, because this was seen as a natural process during groupwork sessions where young people and mentor more or less chose each other. Some of the projects used a combination of both of these matching methods.

In a couple of the projects, mentors were also asked what type of young person they would like to mentor, but some co-ordinators said that they would consider this inappropriate. While some of the project co-ordinators said that they would not match a male mentor with a young woman, others did not consider this type of match at all problematic.

Relationship intensity – length of relationship

In all of the projects, mentors were asked to give a minimum time commitment of six months, although in some projects they were asked for a year. In reality, many mentors stay with projects much longer, although they may take 'time out' between mentoring relationships, sometimes even a few years.

In one of the projects, young people found it frustrating that their relationships were time limited to one year. However, on the other hand, the mentors did not want the relationships to be open-ended in this way, as they found the process exhausting and were content to finish as scheduled.

The peer-mentoring project had an upper age limit for mentors of 23, which was at the behest of the young people, as they did not consider anyone over this age to be their peer!

Boundaries

Boundaries within relationships and their enforcement varied across the projects. What was perfectly acceptable and common practice in one project was quite unacceptable in another. For example, within some projects, it was expected that young people and mentors would have each other's mobile telephone numbers so that they could communicate easily if one or other was delayed for an appointment. However, in other projects, young people were expected to communicate with their mentor only through the project co-ordinator, which created difficulties when mentors met with their young people out of office hours.

All of the projects stated that mentors should not give out their home telephone number or address at all and little detail of their personal or professional lives. Most of the mentors did comply with this rule, although some did share some of their personal history, as they felt this helped them to connect better with the young person.

Another area of difference was in the giving and receiving of gifts within a mentoring relationship. Some projects recommended that only gifts of a token value should be given to young people and that they should not be giving mentors gifts at all. Large items – for example, second-hand furniture – could be given to young people but only through the projects and from the projects.

Visiting young people at home was another area where policy varied widely across the projects. Some co-ordinators advised that only when a mentor and mentee had built up a trusting relationship should the mentor visit young people at home. However, another project accepted that young people and mentors would visit each other frequently at home and that the main part of the mentoring would take place in each other's homes.

As with other aspects of the projects, co-ordinators had modified their stance on boundaries and were moving to a less rigid viewpoint.

As one co-ordinator put it:

> You can't have rigid rules and regulations. 'No young person should ever come to the mentor's house, no young person or mentor should meet in a pub.' You know, I found you actually can't do that because all young people are so different and some will feel more comfortable than others do meeting their mentor in a pub.
>
> What we do is set boundaries around kind of, well, 'have one beer and then go somewhere else', if that's where the young person feels comfortable, as long as they're over 18 there's not a problem with that.
>
> So I think I've learned to become a little bit more laid back and also flexible in how those relationship grow with each other ... I think at the first year I was very clear cut – 'no you can't do that and you can't go here and you can't do this', and it just didn't work.

There were problematic issues, for example, where young people were felt by mentors to be abusing the relationship by using them as a taxi service or meal ticket. Another example was where mentors were in danger of being drawn into the young person's family group rather than remain exclusively there for the young person. Boundary issues were dealt with during the initial training in all of the projects.

Personal advisers and mentors

Under the Children (Leaving Care) Act 2000, it is the responsibility of social services departments to provide young people leaving care with personal advisers. Some of the co-ordinators felt that young people might be unsure about the difference between personal advisers and mentors:

> I think some young people are really confused about who is doing what ... But at the end of the day, if a young person wants a particular thing, they will go to whoever they feel comfortable going to.

There was also a danger of overloading young people with the number of adults involved in their lives:

> Since the introduction of the Leaving Care Act, it has slightly changed, because we are very aware that young people now have personal advisers and it can get a bit confusing about roles.

> So we are aware of not giving the young people too many people, although we still see the mentoring volunteers as playing a very important role in the fact that they are volunteers and not someone they have to see.

With the introduction of the statutory role of personal advisers, some local authorities are reviewing their funding arrangements with mentoring projects that are run in partnership with voluntary organisations. Borough 1 has had the funding it needed to run a mentoring project changed to now fund the delivery of a personal adviser service, with a very different remit. While the local authority does appreciate the value of the project, it has no statutory obligation to provide the service and so is reallocating the funding to personal advisers.

According to the mentoring co-ordinator, the local social services management had originally thought that, as the project was already involved in planning, reviewing and actioning tasks with young people, the mentors could be renamed as personal advisers. However, the co-ordinator has explained the difference in role and function between the mentor and personal adviser. Personal advisers have been recruited separately, with none of the existing volunteer mentors taking up the personal adviser role. The mentors value their voluntary role and feel that these young people appreciate the voluntary commitment of their mentors.

It could be argued that young people are more in control of mentoring relationships than relationships with a personal adviser, as they can choose what they want to do with their mentor. Also, mentors do not automatically have access to young people's files and have no statutory responsibilities. Young people can say what they want to their mentor without that information being discussed at a review. One co-ordinator pointed out that this gives young people time to explore their feelings and attitudes:

> Well, a mentor is very different from other people involved in the young person's life, because, even though they offer a befriending role, they are not the young person's friend, so they are different from friends and family. Hopefully they are also different from a professional worker.

A number of co-ordinators mentioned that sometimes foster carers, parents and residential social workers do not understand the mentoring role. This can cause difficulties in the relationship, as these carers can feel threatened by the mentoring relationship. They may want to know what is discussed between the mentor and young person. Co-ordinators have had to deal sensitively with these difficulties and have been involved in organising information and training sessions for them.

Feedback

All of the project co-ordinators collected feedback about the service from young people in some way, either directly or indirectly. This contributed to some kind of quality control and allowed co-ordinators to develop the service to meet the needs of its users. Some of the mentors collected written feedback, although generally this kind of feedback was not very successfully collected. Where co-ordinators were able to talk to the young people after the relationship ended this was more successful, although they did not necessarily record this information but used it for development purposes. Where young people have terminated mentoring relationships early it has been more difficult for co-ordinators to get feedback.

Feedback is collected from mentors on an ongoing basis through individual and group supervision sessions. Where mentors complete log sheets of their interaction with their young people this also contributes to the feedback.

Key points

■ Mentoring projects were developed in response to the vulnerability of young people leaving care during their journey to adulthood. Their isolation, lack of support, possible mental health problems and the need for additional services at the time of transition were all cited as reasons.

■ The main type of mentoring was one-to-one, but this included adult and peer mentoring.

■ Mentoring relationships were likely to include both 'instrumental' task-focused and 'expressive' befriending roles, although there were differences in emphasis between projects and there was no uniform development from one of these dimensions to the other.

■ Most of the mentoring projects were either based in specialist leaving care teams or had developed links with them.

- The projects were funded by the Prince's Trust for the recruitment, training and supervision of mentors (all projects) and by different partnership arrangements between local authorities and voluntary organisations. All funding was short-term and seen by most project leaders as inadequate.

- Most of the projects had well-developed systems for mentor selection, training, support, matching and feedback.

- Problematic areas included: the impact of defined time limits on young people; boundaries within mentoring relationships – these varied across the projects; and confusion between mentors and personal advisers appointed under the Children (Leaving Care) Act 2000.

Note

1 Longer-term mentoring and mentoring longer-term as defined in Chapter 1, the current study, page 7.

3 Young people and their mentors: the database sample

This chapter is based on information about our mentoring relationships gathered from a file search in 13 of the projects. The database comprised 181 mentoring relationships, although, as mentioned in Chapter 1, not all of these contained complete information. The file search included information from: referral forms; information gathered to facilitate the matching process; session logs or recording sheets completed by mentors after each time they met with the young person; evaluation forms completed by young people; and comments or summaries written by project workers. Our analysis starts by presenting a profile of the young people and their mentors. This is followed by a description of the different components of the mentoring process.

Profile of the young people

Gender ($n = 179$)

The database sample of mentoring relationships was balanced between males and females, with just over half (51 per cent, 91) being male and 49 per cent (88) female ($n = 179$).

Age ($n = 167$)

The average (mode) age was 17 ($n = 167$) and the young people ranged from 15 to 23 years of age when they started being mentored (see Figure 1). In many of the projects, there was a policy to begin mentoring between 16 and 21 years of age.

Figure 1 Age

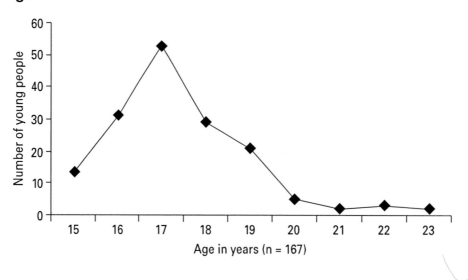

Ethnic origin (n = 172)

The majority, over three-quarters (76 per cent, 131), of the young people were white in origin with only 6 per cent (11) of mixed heritage and 16 per cent (28) black young people (see Figure 2). There is no directly comparable data in terms of national figures.

Figure 2 Ethnic origin

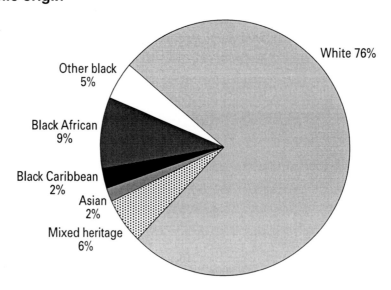

Figure 3 Distribution of young people among projects (*n* = 181)

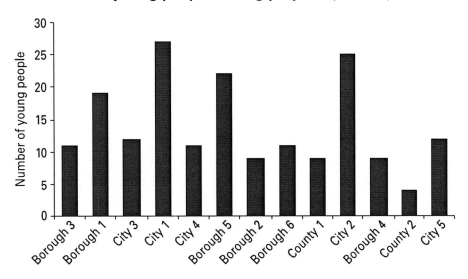

As can be seen from Figure 3, different numbers of young people were included in our sample across the projects.

Preferences

In most of the projects, prior to be being matched, young people were able to specify certain criteria they would like their mentor to meet. Sixty-two (59 per cent, *n* = 105) of the young people wanted their mentor to match certain criteria. Nearly half (47 per cent, *n* = 103) wanted a male or female in particular, and over one-third (35 per cent, *n* = 103) requested a mentor in a particular age group. A few (7 per cent, *n* = 103) asked for a mentor from a particular ethnic group. This was mainly young refugees who wanted someone they could speak to in their mother tongue and also so that they could keep in touch with their own culture.

Profile of the mentors

Nearly three-quarters of the mentors were female (73 per cent, 103), which reflects the findings of other research that shows that social care mentoring is a predominantly female occupation (see Figure 4).

Figure 4 Mentor gender (*n* = 141)

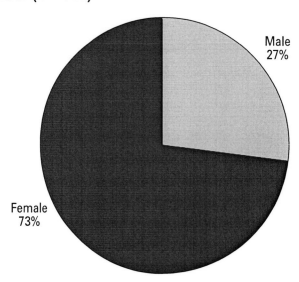

The mentors ranged in age between 18 and 62 years old with the mean age being 34 (*n* = 105). Mentors had a wide age range, although two-fifths (41 per cent) were under the age of 30 and nearly two-thirds (63 per cent) were under the age of 40 (see Figure 5).

Figure 5 Mentor age range (*n* = 105)

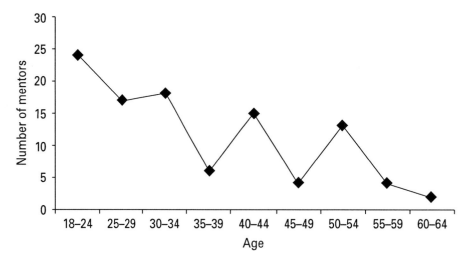

More than three-quarters of the mentors were white British, although many other ethnic groups were represented among the mentors included on the database. Figures 6 and 7 show the range of backgrounds of these mentors. Figure 7 shows the minority ethnic groups in more detail.

Figure 6 Mentor ethnic origin (*n* = 112)

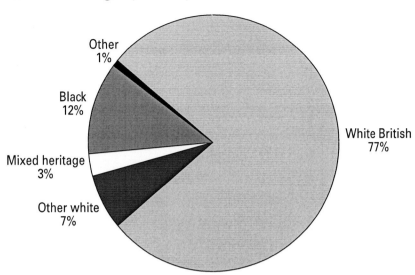

Figure 7 Mentor minority ethnic origin (*n* = 25)

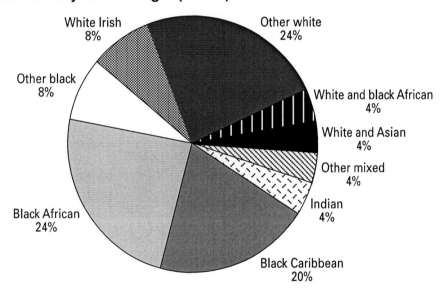

*Mentor occupation (*n* = 115)*

Nearly three-quarters of the mentors (70 per cent, 80) were in employment – full-time, part-time or self-employed – when they started mentoring and 15 (13 per cent) were in education or training. These two groups in particular already had busy lives when they took on the challenges and responsibilities of mentoring a young care leaver. Sixteen (14 per cent) were not in employment or education, which included both those unemployed and full-time homemakers. Two of the mentors were retired and two were full-time carers (see Figure 8).

Figure 8 Mentor occupation (*n* = 115)

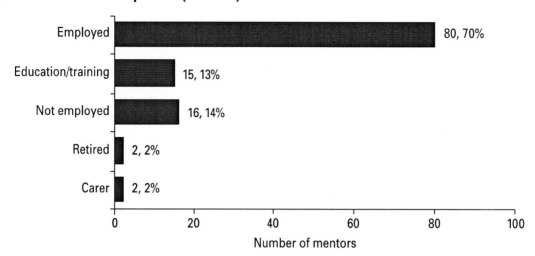

Referral

*Number of weeks young people waited before matching (*n* = 102)*

A small number of the young people were matched with their mentors as soon as they were referred to the projects, but, at the other extreme, some young people waited up to a year from referral. Although this sounds as if they were left without a service for a long time, this may not have been the case. Some of the young people were still involved in the mentoring projects although not engaged in one-to-one mentoring. This was particularly the case in the peer-mentoring project where many young people were involved in group work. Some of the young people did have to wait until enough mentors were recruited and trained before they could be matched, and sometimes they had to wait for an appropriate mentor to be recruited. The mean length of time between referral and matching was 11.54 weeks. (Criminal Records Bureau changes in application procedure during this time also increased the waiting time.)

More than two-fifths of the young people (42 per cent, 43) were matched within one month of referral and nearly two-thirds were matched within two months (61 per cent, 62). This suggests that most of the young people did not have a protracted wait for support at such an important stage of their lives (see Figure 9).

Figure 9 Number of weeks waited before matching (*n* = 102)

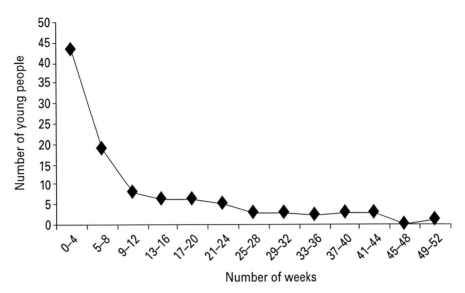

Number of weeks

Reasons for referral (n = 115)

Figure 10 shows the reasons why young people were referred or referred themselves to the mentoring projects. Some of the young people were referred to the projects for more than one reason.

Figure 10 Reasons for referral

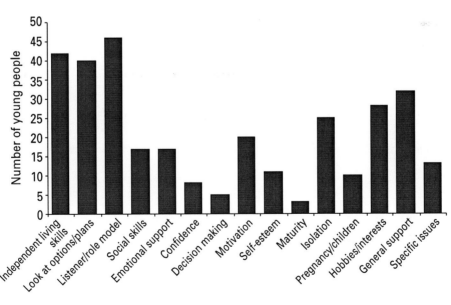

Where young people's reasons for wanting a mentor were kept on the file, a comparison showed that these were very similar to the referral reasons, which suggest that referrers consulted with young people prior to submitting the referral.

Planning and goal setting

Although the projects encouraged mentors to draw up action plans with their young people either at the start or soon after the start of relationships, few of these were in the files. Thirty action plans were examined and it was found that nearly half (14) were concerned with supporting the young person with education or employment, 12 with improving independent living skills and 11 with developing hobbies and interests. Nine of the action plans were concerned with building up the young people's social skills and seven were for the mentor to listen to the young person and to be someone they could talk to. Other areas covered were for support around relationships, cultural issues and helping the young person to consider their future.

Although there were action plans for only 30 of the young people, individual goals that were not formally recorded were often set in each mentoring plan. This could be gleaned from the mentor's log sheets and reflected the reasons why the young people were referred. The areas covered included the areas mentioned in the action plans and reduction in offending behaviour, managing accommodation, building social networks, confidence and self-esteem.

Mentor activity

Mentors worked with young people on a number of areas in their lives and usually on more than one simultaneously. Figure 11 shows this activity.

Figure 11 Areas mentors worked on with young people

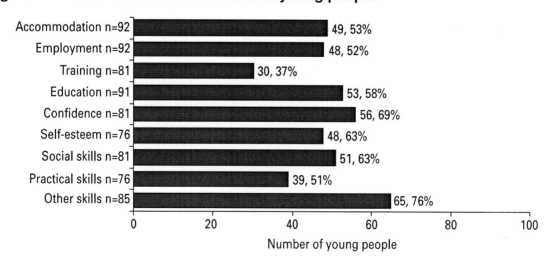

N numbers indicate number of cases where data was available.

In over half of the mentoring relationships (53 per cent), young people worked with their mentor on accommodation. A similar proportion (52 per cent) worked on employment, over one-third (37 per cent) on training and 58 per cent on education. Mentors also addressed the areas of confidence (69 per cent) and self-esteem (63 per cent). Social skills (63 per cent) and practical skills (51 per cent) were also key areas in the mentoring relationship.

Outcomes

The following outcome data relates to the outcomes at the end of the mentoring relationship (n = 169) or at the stage of the file search where the relationship was ongoing (n = 12). Files generally do not contain updates of what happens with the young person at any time after the relationship finishes. Most of the projects did not operate a follow-up policy, although many allowed young people to be re-referred to them. Where projects restricted the length of the mentoring relationship, if a young person still needed support, they were matched with another mentor. This could happen several times according to the young person's needs.

Achievement of goals

'Achievement of goals' was a qualitative measure assessed by the researcher while carrying out the file search. Evidence was collated from mentors' log sheets, comments by project co-ordinators and workers, and young people's feedback where this was available.

Goals that the young people were aiming to achieve through mentoring were mainly, although not exclusively, centred around their move to independent living from foster or residential care. For some, the goals were very specific and mentors and their young people aimed to work through these on a week-by-week basis. The mentor would telephone their young person between meetings to check that these tasks had been completed. However, many of the tasks were of a less specific nature. Many of the young people were aiming to develop their independent living skills. This included budgeting skills and cooking as well as looking after their accommodation and coping with independent living in general. Finding or changing their accommodation was the goal of some of the young people.

Some of the young parents had goals that included accessing childcare with the aim of finding work or returning to college. However, a number of the goals related to specific employment, for example a number of the young men were hoping to join the army. Building social networks was an area that young people were keen to develop. Others had specific small goals around literacy, numeracy, study skills and revision plans, while others wanted help to look at their educational options. Other goals mentioned included 'staying off drugs', building confidence and self-esteem, 'stopping offending' and learning to swim!

For some young people, their goals were to become involved in some form of leisure activity, usually to help prevent isolation and to build social networks, although for some they just needed a companion. One young person wanted to be able to rediscover and build on his cultural background through mentoring.

Although the stated goal may not have been achieved and no other goal achieved either, the young person may still have had a positive outcome. There were some positive aspects to outcomes for most of the young people. Where it was known whether the stated goals had been achieved (n = 86), three-quarters of the young people achieved their goals (76 per cent, 65). Thirty-two (52 per cent, n = 62) of the young people had achieved other goals that emerged during the relationship. Of those who did not achieve their original goal (21), seven achieved another goal (see Table 1).

Positive outcomes (n = 115)

While achievement of goals represented an instrumental outcome for the young people, positive outcomes included more expressive outcomes. Forty-three of the relationships had planned endings, although some of these were relatively short relationships focused around a particular goal. Where outcomes were known (n = 115), more than four-fifths (107, 93 per cent) did have at least some positive outcomes by the end of the mentoring relationship. Eight young people had no positive outcomes and it was unclear for five others.

Table 1 Goals achieved during the mentoring relationship

Goals achieved		%	Other goals		%
Yes	65	76	Yes	32	52
No	21	24	No	30	48
Total	86	100	Total	62	100

In general, mentoring relationships had positive outcomes consistent with young people's goals. However, for many of the young people, having someone to talk to who was there specifically for them was a positive outcome, as they had no one to fulfil this role in the past.

Positive outcomes included the development of a young person's confidence and self-esteem, and an improvement in their ability to sustain relationships. Young people also had positive outcomes in terms of their education, whether this was achieving in examinations or being able to complete their schooling or get a place in college. Gaining independent living skills, practical and social skills were also recorded as positive outcomes for the young people. For some of the young people, positive outcomes included a reduction in offending behaviour or other behaviour such as self-harming.

New skills that contributed to the positive outcome of the mentoring relationship were often developed in the course of the relationship. These new skills included independent living skills, communication and assertiveness, as well as skills in terms of particular leisure interests or literacy.

Negative outcomes (n = 96)

Where known, half of the relationships had some kind of negative outcome, although, for many of these, there were also positive outcomes in the relationships as well. Negative outcomes were sometimes just that the young person had left the project and the ending was unplanned. However, prior to that stage, positive outcomes may have been achieved. Some of the mentoring relationships did not get properly established where the young people missed several mentoring meetings, or where the mentor and young person did not engage. Two of the young people were asylum seekers whose asylum claim was subsequently rejected. For some other young people, despite the additional support, their lives became chaotic.

Forty-four (37 per cent, $n = 118$) of the relationships had unplanned endings. Nineteen of the mentoring relationships had unplanned endings because the young person was missing appointments. For some, this was because their lives had become too chaotic, others were no longer interested in the support offered. Some mentors found this aspect of their behaviour particularly difficult to deal with. In nine of the relationships where the ending was unplanned, the mentor withdrew and no longer met with and supported the young person. In some of these cases, the young person could be rematched but inevitably felt let down by someone they were learning to trust. Three of the relationships ended early, as the mentor did not feel they were progressing. Three ended because the young person did not engage with the mentor. Two ended when the young people developed challenging mental health problems and two when young people had serious problems with substance abuse.

Impact

The areas that were worked on by mentors with their young people did not necessarily lead to positive outcomes in that area by the end of the relationship. For example, the mentor of one young woman spent time with her dealing with budgeting, relationships and practical and social skills, as well as confidence and self-esteem. The reported positive outcomes for the young person included a large variety of social skills, including leadership, motivation, tolerance, problem solving, caring for others, managing a project, responsibility, setting and achieving goals, in addition to budgeting and independent living skills.

One young person who felt their initial goals had not been met (these included education, employment, developing hobbies and finding alternative accommodation) had nevertheless improved her parenting skills and accessed local childcare services and parenting agencies. She had also trained in interview skills and sat on the interview panel for mentors. She had realistic plans for the future and developed her communication skills.

Planning for the future (n = 181)

A positive aspect of many of the mentoring relationships was that, by the end of them, young people were making at least some plans for their future. Seventy of the young people were known to have made some such plans. Unfortunately, much of this data was not available in the files and could be gleaned only from the mentor's recording sheets.

Of the whole sample ($n = 181$), 17 (9 per cent) of the young people were known to have made some plans around accommodation and just under one-fifth (32, 18 per cent) had made some plans for their employment. Much smaller proportions (seven, 4 per cent and 16, 9 per cent respectively) had made plans around training and/or education. Some of the young people wanted to help others and 13 (7 per cent) had made plans to do some kind of voluntary work; for some, this was mentoring. One-tenth (18, 10 per cent) were planning to do something for their personal development and 19 (11 per cent) had made some other kinds of plan for their future. Some young people's plans covered several of these areas (see Figure 12).

Figure 12 Young people's future plans (*n* = 181)

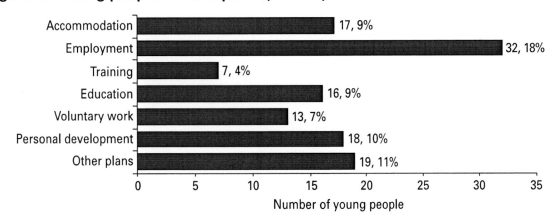

Length of relationships (n = 76)

The data on the length of the relationships was gleaned from the files using a combination of the recording sheets, correspondence and other records. The information is not officially collected or recorded. The number of cases where this information was available was only 76 (42 per cent of the data sample) and, of these, the number of weeks of the relationship ranged from two to 132. The mode time was one year and the mean number of weeks was 33. A number of the projects operated a policy of time limiting each mentoring relationships to one year, but, where a young person needed continuing support after this time, they were matched with another mentor. This could happen more than once and, within the research period, six of the young people each had two mentoring relationships and one had three. Some of the young people in the current sample may also have been matched with a mentor and ended the relationship prior to the research period and this will not have been recorded (see Table 2).

Young people met with their mentors between one and 100 times over the above period, with the mean number of meetings being 19.

Table 2 Length of mentoring relationships

Length of relationship	Frequency	Valid %
Up to six months	40	48
Six months to one year	26	31
Over one year	18	21
Total	84	100

Were there any significant links?

Gender

Male mentors were far more likely to be matched with young men and young women were more likely to be matched with female mentors. Five young women were matched with male mentors and 54 per cent (37) (*n* = 139) young men with female mentors.

Mentors were slightly more likely to work with young men on accommodation matters (but not significantly) and also with regard to training. Gender did not appear to be a factor linked to any other aspect of mentors' work with young people.

Ethnic origin

Statistical tests carried out on the data showed that the mentoring experience of young people was very similar in terms of their ethnic origin. No significance was found in what mentors worked on with young people, goals achieved, future plans of young people, negative outcomes or the length of the relationship. Ethnic origin also had no effect on the length of the relationships.

Neither the young person's gender nor their ethnic origin had any statistically significant impact on the length of a mentoring relationship.

Age

There was no relationship between achievement of goals and age of the young person. There was, however, a slight tendency among those in the older age group of 19–22 to have fewer negative outcomes than those aged 18 or under. A young person's age had no impact when considering young people's plans for the future.

Longer-term mentoring

Although not statistically significant, the length of time a mentoring relationship continues does seem to have some impact on certain outcome areas. Young people who had been mentored for over a year were more likely to have plans for the future during the course of their relationship (see Table 3).

There were indications that goals – original and other – were more likely to be achieved in a relationship that lasts over six months. Also that young people were slightly less likely to have negative outcomes when they were mentored for a longer period. They were also more likely to have a plan for the future when they were mentored for over a year.

Similarly, young people were most likely to have achieved their original goals when mentored for over one year and least likely to achieve them when mentored for less than six months (see Table 4).

A similar pattern emerges when looking at other goals that were established through the course of the relationship and were achieved by the end (see Table 5).

The longer the mentoring relationship was, the more likely it would be that positive outcomes would result (see Table 6). Unplanned endings often happened early in the relationships. So, once relationships had been established with young people, unless they faced a crisis or needed to move away, endings could be planned. In longer-term mentoring, the relationship between the young person and the mentor had developed into one of trust and both were working towards achieving the goals.

Table 3 Length of relationship by future plans

| Length of relationship | Future plans | | | | Total | |
| | Yes | | No | | | |
	No.	%	No.	%	No.	%
Up to six months	18	64.3	10	35.7	28	100.0
Six months to one year	14	82.4	3	17.6	17	100.0
Over one year	14	100.0			14	100.0
Total	46	78.0	13	22.0	59	100.0

Table 4 Length of relationship by goals achieved

| Length of relationship | Goal achieved | | | | Total | |
| | Yes | | No | | | |
	No.	%	No.	%	No.	%
Up to six months	15	51.7	14	48.3	29	100
Six months to one year	16	94.1	1	5.9	17	100
Over one year	8	88.9	1	11.1	9	100
Total	39	70.9	16	29.1	55	100

Table 5 Length of relationship by other goals achieved

Length of relationship	Other goals achieved				Total	
	Yes		No			
	No.	%	No.	%	No.	%
Up to six months	6	25.0	18	75.0	24	100
Six months to one year	3	25.0	9	75.0	12	100
Over one year	7	100			7	100
Total	16	37.2	27	62.8	43	100

Table 6 Length of relationship by positive outcome

Length of relationship	Positive outcome				Total	
	Yes		No			
	No.	%	No.	%	No.	%
Up to six months	25	86.2	4	13.8	29	100
Six months to one year	23	100.0			23	100
Over one year	16	100.0			16	100
Total	64	94.1	4	5.9	68	100

The corollary of this is that shorter relationships were slightly more likely to end with negative outcomes (see Table 7).

Table 7 Length of relationship by negative outcome

Length of relationship	Negative outcome				Total	
	Yes		No			
	No.	%	No.	%	No.	%
Up to six months	17	63.0	10	37.0	27	100
Six months to one year	8	47.1	9	52.9	17	100
Over one year	3	33.3	6	66.7	9	100
Total	28	52.8	25	47.2	53	100

Key points

■ Projects work with similar numbers of young men and young women, aged between 15 and 23. Just over three-quarters are white and 22 per cent are black or mixed-heritage young people.

■ Most mentors are female (three-quarters), aged between 18 and 62. Just over three-quarters were white British, the remaining quarter includes black, Asian, mixed-heritage and 'other white' mentors. Just under three-quarters were in employment.

■ Most young people (two-thirds) were matched with a mentor within two months and they were referred, or referred themselves, for a wide variety of reasons. Wanting a 'listener' or 'role model', help with 'independent living skills', exploring their 'options and plans' and 'general support' were the most cited reasons.

■ Mentors worked with young people on both 'instrumental' and 'expressive' areas. The former included education, employment and training, and practical skills, and the latter confidence and self-esteem.

■ Information on outcomes from the database was measured in two ways. First, where information was available, just over three-quarters of young people 'achieved their goals' and over half had achieved other goals that emerged during the mentoring relationship. Second, most young people (93 per cent) had some 'positive outcome' recorded by the end of the mentoring relationship. This included either an 'instrumental' goal achievement or a more 'expressive' dimension, such as improving their confidence or ability to sustain relationships.

■ Half of the relationships had some negative outcomes, which included lack of engagement, missing appointments and unplanned endings – often linked to chaotic lives. However, where young people had unplanned endings, some had achieved positive outcomes prior to that time.

■ Around half the cases where information was available had unplanned endings. While, in nearly half of those cases, relationships ended because of young people missing appointments, in a fifth of these cases, the mentor withdrew and no longer met with and supported the young person.

■ Young people who were mentored for over a year were more likely to have achieved their original goals and to have future plans. Also, the longer the mentoring relationship lasted, the greater the likelihood of a positive outcome was.

4 The mentoring relationship: the views of young people and their mentors

Why did you want a mentor?

Someone to talk to when I need to.

This chapter is based on interviews with 17 young people – those who were mentored for more than six months and those whose mentoring relationships had ended between two and four years before we interviewed them – and their mentors. Following a profile of the sample, we explore the mentoring process, including matching young people with mentors, the reasons why young people were referred to the projects and why they wanted a mentor, as well as their plans and goals.

Profile of the interview sample

Of the 17 young people interviewed, nine were female and eight were male. Nine of the young people described themselves as white, four as black African, two as black Caribbean, one as British Caribbean mixed and one as black British (see Figure 13).

Figure 13 Ethnic origin (*n* = 17)

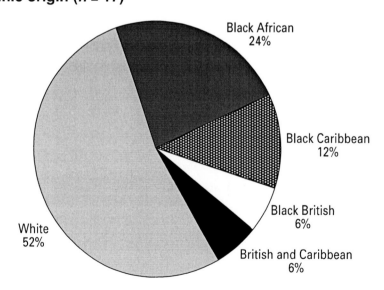

At the time of interview, the young people's ages ranged from 19 to 27, and the mean age was 20. Two of the young people had learning difficulties and one a specific learning difficulty. One of the young people was suffering from mental illness requiring ongoing treatment and at least a further two young people had suffered mental health problems that required treatment.

Comparison with database sample

How representative was our sample? While the proportion of males and females in each sample was not dissimilar, the ethnic make-up of the two groups was considerably different. There were proportionately more black young people among those we interviewed than in the database sample. This is accounted for by the inclusion of one project in particular, which was working with a high proportion of black young people.

Age

The young people in the sample that we interviewed were in the age range 16 to 22, whereas the young people in the database sample were aged 15 to 23 when they started being mentored. The most common age (mode) for those interviewed was 18 at the start of mentoring whereas, for the database sample, it was 17.

Proportionately more of the interview sample than the database sample had been matched for more than a year. This can be explained by the fact that those young people who had ongoing relationships or relatively long mentoring relationships were more likely to have stayed in touch with their project. In addition, one of the mentoring projects included in the interviews had a particularly high proportion of longer-term relationships. Another project that was included, however, restricted mentoring relationships to one year only. One of the young people in the interviewed group had a series of one-year mentoring relationships.

Nearly one-third (30 per cent, five) of the young people we interviewed had a peer mentor compared with 7 per cent (12) in the database sample.

Circumstances at the time of interview

Eleven of the young people were living in their own tenancies, two were living with relatives and four in semi-independent accommodation. Seven were living with their partners at least for part of the time. Six of the young people were parents by this point in their lives and one young woman was pregnant with her first child. Two of the young mothers were unhappy with their accommodation and were hoping to transfer from flats to houses at some point. One other young woman was hoping to move to larger accommodation, but felt she needed to set that wish against making another move just for the sake of it. She felt that she had made many moves while in care and was anxious for some stability. All of the other young people were happy with their accommodation, although did not necessarily plan to stay where they were living in the long term. One young person was planning to move away in the near future, as he was hoping to join the army.

At the time of the interview, only four of the young people were in full-time work. Five were officially unemployed, two were unable to work because of mental health issues, four were full-time parents, one was a full-time carer and one was studying.

By the time they were interviewed, all of the young people were in contact with professionals who they could go to for support. Six of the young people still had social work support, either for themselves or for their children. Eight were still in contact with the mentoring project.

When asked whom they would talk to if they needed further support, eight said they would talk to a friend or partner. Four would speak to a relative and six would seek support from professionals. Five young people said they would talk to their mentor even though not all were still officially being mentored. Six of the young people had active ongoing relationships with their mentors at this time, although three of these had different mentors than those they were seeing during the research period.

Why a mentor?

The young people who were interviewed were all referred to the mentoring projects for some kind of additional support during their transition from care to independence. For some, this was a transition complicated through pregnancy, isolation, lack of independent living skills or low self-esteem and motivation. The support needed was around different aspects of transition. This included the process of gaining employment, independent living skills, gaining or improving social skills, parenting skills, relationships and self-esteem. The young people expressed this need for support in different ways when requesting a mentor, and many said they wanted someone to talk to who would be there for them and support them in whatever way they felt they needed:

> … when I am really upset there is someone there, help me sort out my problems. Someone to talk to when I'm down, money problems, college.
> (Hayley)

One young man wanted a mentor 'just in case' and had seen how a mentor had supported his friend during the period of transition to independence:

> … in case I need one – in case I get kicked out of the [housing project], in case I need someone to speak to.
> (Lee)

Choices

Although not all of the young people had specifically requested a mentor, they all made an active choice to be mentored once the suggestion was made to them. This was usually by a professional worker already involved with them, for example, social worker, aftercare worker or a friend who was already being mentored, or, as in one case, a relative who was being mentored.

However, some of the young people reported that they did not recall being asked if they had any preferences about the characteristics of their mentor. Those at the peer-mentoring project reported that they were not able to request preferences, but most of these had already met with their mentor and knew them before they were matched. As with all the other projects, if they did not wish to proceed with a particular mentor, they were free to do this and could be rematched.

In terms of how mentors and young people spent their time together, in general the young people set the agenda, although sometimes this meant that the mentor made suggestions and the young person chose from those.

Matching

In order for a successful relationship to be established, careful matching of the mentor and young person needed to take place. Two of the young people commented that it meant a lot to them that they felt able to trust their mentors very early on in their relationship. Both of these were young women who had experienced difficulties with parenting their children and felt that the mentors they were matched with were particularly appropriate:

> I talked to her quite a bit because I could open up to her. I really did trust her so I could talk to her about anything.
> (Vanessa)

> The first day I met her I really started opening up to her cos I just knew in myself that she was the one!
> (Tracey)

Although mentors were not encouraged to have preferences, Pauline had requested to work with a young mother, as she felt she had more to offer to a young woman in this position as she had children herself.

Gender and ethnicity

While some projects had a policy of never matching a male mentor with a young woman, this was not always the case. Gender did emerge from the interviews as an important issue for some of the young people. Six of the young men had female mentors and two of the young women had male mentors. One of the young men had specifically requested a female mentor, as he had difficulties in talking to women and by the time he was interviewed he felt that this was no longer a problem.

Another young man, Nat, appreciated that his mentor was female as he saw her as a kind of mother figure. He felt alone and isolated from his cultural roots, as well as his family. Also, it was important to him that his mentor was from the same ethnic background and was able to help him to feel 'at home':

> The most important help for me was having somebody to talk to about my problems. About being alone, and missing my parents. And just not being sure about why I were, or if I'm good enough to do something. That's what I question always. It was the lowest point of my life.

> If the mentor was a man I don't know how much more it would have
> helped. But it definitely helped that, in a way that is not sexual or
> anything, but just really the attention of what I was lacking, which is a
> woman, mother or whatever. So it was helpful.
> (Nat)

One of the young women initially felt anxious about being matched with a male
mentor. She was referred specifically to help her express her feelings and needed a
mentor who would be able to listen to her and respond appropriately:

> I felt a bit … I don't know what's the word … Cos he was a man and I
> would rather speak to a woman about stuff. And he was my first one and I
> was very nervous to speak to him … We was chatting about stuff and that
> but it wasn't the same as like whenever I've talked to a woman.
> (Hayley)

That is not to say that Hayley did not feel supported by her mentor, but she did not
feel able to discuss her personal history with him:

> I think I would have got on a lot better with a woman than a man.

Her mentor too had expressed reservations about being matched with a young
woman, as he thought it would be difficult to strike up a relationship with a teenage
girl, coming as he did from a male-dominated working environment. In practice, he
felt that the relationship worked well, although he was unsure what Hayley got from it
and sometimes he did feel a bit awkward.

Over time, Hayley recognised that her mentor had been very supportive to her by
helping her with personal difficulties she was having at the time, as well as while she
was at college. She used to look forward to his visits and enjoyed the fact he was
someone different:

> I did really enjoy it, it was good. And he helped a lot. Like he tried his best
> when it was stuff that it was weird for him to answer. But he still tried. He
> gave the best to it.
> (Hayley)

Another young woman who had been allocated a male mentor had no problem
herself but her boyfriend found the situation difficult to deal with until he had met the
mentor and talked with him:

> It was like having a girlfriend around. My partner was not always happy. I just said to him. No, he is my mentor. I don't see him in that kind of way.
> (Kate)

Kate was already well prepared for independence but had wanted a mentor because she felt that she had a lot going on in her life, being pregnant and moving to her own flat. Her mentor supported her pregnancy by taking her shopping and going with her to antenatal classes when her boyfriend was unavailable. Her mentor did not express any difficulties with being matched with a young woman. However, he had initially requested to work with a young man with difficulties as he was 'looking for a challenge'!

Kate felt that matching was an important factor in the success of a mentoring relationship. Although she did not think that having a male mentor was a problem, she did feel that they had little in common and that she would have been able to relate to him better if he had been in care himself:

> I think that when they interview mentors they should find out a little bit more about who you are and what you do and match the right mentor to the right person ... Me and [mentor] didn't really have that much in common
> (Kate)

Planning and goal setting

Mentors were encouraged to construct action plans with the young people at the beginning of the mentoring relationship, although this was emphasised in some projects more than others. Mentors in these projects were working with, rather than on, young people, and relationships depended on co-operation and negotiation between both parties.

Tracey was clear about the planning carried out with her mentor:

> What you done was, you sat down and discussed what it is you actually wanted to achieve and what your goals were, and then we would aim towards that.
> (Tracey)

Her mentor, Suzanne, was clear about her role in helping Tracey to set and manage her own goals, although she often felt frustrated when Tracey seemed to thwart the successful completion of some of the goals:

> There's no point in sitting there and saying, 'These should be your goals'.
> I very quickly realised that the young person has to want the goals. My
> job as I saw it was to support them on the goals they wanted.
> (Suzanne)

While not all of the young people felt that they had had an action plan, a number of them did recall having goals they were working towards in their mentoring relationship, which were subject to change.

The young people were going through a transition period, and their lives were subject to frequent and sometimes rapid changes at this time. Those who had managed to include goals in their action plan found that they could not always achieve these and, conversely, new goals would often emerge. Catherine's pregnancy part way through the mentoring relationship meant that her goals changed from just dealing with the transition to independent living, to preparation for parenting. Danielle's main goal was thwarted, as she developed a mental illness, but other smaller goals emerged and she was satisfied that her action plan had been followed:

> [Mentor] came up with a lot of ideas of how to get there and what to do. If
> there was anything on my mind I could ask her and she would explain.
> (Danielle)

One mentor rather enthusiastically tried to put together a personal development plan for his young person but was sensitive enough to abandon this when it did not appeal.

Intensity

Within the interview sample, the young people had been mentored for a period of six months to over three years and three of these were ongoing relationships at the time of the interview.

Meetings lasted from between about one hour to about half a day if the mentor felt the young person needed to be around that long. One of the projects did specify that meetings should last no longer than two hours. This restriction was in place to prevent exploitation of the mentors by the young people and also to ensure that mentors were clear about the level of commitment expected from them:

> If you are a mentor you should be there for the kids. The same way as you were there for your kids, whenever they want you. I felt I had to be available. OK occasionally I couldn't stay.
> (Pauline)

Pauline had a close relationship with her young person and strongly felt she should be available to support her, as she had complex needs, as well as a young family to look after. In addition to having learning difficulties, her young person also had to cope with separating from her partner and her children being temporarily placed in care. Pauline would see her on average once a week, unless she was in crisis, in which case she would see her as many as three times a week. She also made herself available by telephone through the mentoring project, but did not share personal contact details with her, following project guidelines:

> She felt that OK I wasn't letting her down. Because I was very aware of her view of social services and social workers as well. There they are supposedly doing their all and then they get promoted and bugger off. 'How worthwhile am I that they have left?' That was one thing about mentoring, to be honest, that I did think was important about it. As a constant.

Pauline's mentee valued this level of support at a difficult time in her life and felt that, if she had not had a mentor, she would not have shared her difficulties, including domestic violence, with anyone. One of the most important things for her about her mentoring experience was that she felt she could trust her mentor and knew she would be there for her whenever she needed support:

> She was there with me for the appointments and if I didn't understand it she would explain it all afterwards and she would take notes of everything while we were there.
> (Vanessa)

One of the other mentors found that the project guidelines with regard to sharing telephone numbers were far too restrictive to enable him to work with his young person and develop a trusting relationship:

> The strict rules are that you mustn't give anything away about yourself,
> etc., etc., and you mustn't give mobile phones and they can't contact you.
> But none of that works in practice, I don't think anyway.
>
> Because how you can have a … fairly trusting open relationship if you are
> withholding things like mobile numbers. So [young person] has my mobile
> numbers and we have established really that he should drop me a line if
> he can't make it.

His mentee, Lee, appreciated this level of contact and, although he met with his
mentor weekly, he did contact him by telephone if he needed anything.

The mentoring experience

Mentors and their young people did a variety of activities together that depended on
the needs of the young person as well as their goals. For three of the young people
who had young children, mentors tended to visit them in their homes and activities
were chosen that were suitable for including the child. For one mentor, this involved
teaching the young parent how to play with, and read to, her children. This mentor
also tried to help the young person by giving her hints and tips about looking after
her flat:

> Shopping, hospital appointments, nursery … Out with the kids. She'd
> help me with the kids. Like if I was there sorting out [child A] she would sit
> there and read a book with [child B] and play with [child B] if I needed to
> sort [child A] out.

Although project guidelines often stated that meetings should take place on so-called
neutral ground, sometimes mentors and project co-ordinators were prepared to
negotiate on an individual basis in order to meet the needs of the young person.
Another mentor needed to meet the young person at her home, as she was
agoraphobic at the start of her mentoring relationship. Part of the work done was to
help her go to local shopping areas and use buses:

> At first she used to come round and talk to me. Take me shopping to try
> and get me to go out on buses instead of being too scared to go out. She
> used to help me phone around to sort all my bills out. She helped me to
> keep my flat together to keep it clean and tidy. She took me to any
> appointments I needed to go to help me build up my confidence.
> [Tracey]

By the end of the relationship, the young person was able to use public transport confidently and had joined some local groups of young people.

While many of the activities shared by mentors and young people may appear to be ordinary, everyday activities with no particular purpose, this belied the opportunities these activities gave for young people to talk to their mentors and for trusting relationships to be built up. Such opportunities arose during shopping trips, going to cafes and burger bars, going to the pub and sharing a sporting activity.

Young people and their mentors talked mainly about themselves and their views of life and what had happened to them. They talked about things they needed, such as employment or housing advice or help with literacy. When a crisis happened, they would often discuss that with their mentor too.

In traditional one-to-one mentoring, mentors were encouraged not to share anything about themselves with their young people, although one of the mentors we interviewed found that he had a better relationship with his young person when he did share a little about his own experiences. Some of the projects had a flexible approach in that mentors were expected to make clear decisions about what they shared with their mentor, why and what impact this may have on future work they do with the young person.

However, the rationale of peer mentoring was that the mentor sharing their experience of care, leaving care and after care – the throughcare process – could help young people. It was in this way that the mentor would be a role model for the young person. Other projects saw the mentor role as presenting young people with different options for their behaviour and development.

What makes a mentor special for a young person?

The young people valued the more informal approach of their mentors – they did not take a distanced professional stance with them. They were seen as more accessible than their social workers and less judgemental. Many of the young people commented that they appreciated their level of accessibility to their mentor. For some young people this meant they could contact them whenever they felt they needed to. This was not always the case, as many of the projects advised mentors not to give out their contact details:

> He doesn't have like a specific time like 9 to 5 when he works, like a
> social worker. You can only phone them at certain times. [Mentor]'s
> always there you know. You can phone them any time.
> (Kate)

One young woman, Danielle, had 11 different people involved in her life when she
was being mentored. But, to her, the mentor was very different to these:

> It was more friendly contact than professional. She never used to dress
> up in a suit ... She just used to be very friendly. It was helpful because
> you could talk to her about anything and she wouldn't have any problems
> about it.

> It's not because they take you out or anything like that. It's because they
> explain things in a better way than professionals would. They help you to
> cope with certain situations.
> (Danielle)

They also appreciated that their mentor was there for them exclusively:

> It felt like there was someone for me, someone that is not your partner or
> friend.
> (Kate)

One young woman who had a peer mentor felt that it was very important to have a
mentor who had similar experiences to herself in terms of being in and leaving care:

> I think if I never had a mentor I wouldn't have turned out the way I've
> turned out now ... Cos having someone there that you know is there for
> you. No, not like a social worker cos my experience of social workers is
> that they let you down.

> So having her there and knowing she's been through everything I'm
> going through now, you know ... it's different like that, I have more
> respect for her.
> (Clarice)

Kirsty was pregnant with her first child when she was referred to the mentoring
project by her social worker for extra support. She was unprepared for independent
living and had to move from a relative when she became pregnant:

She wasn't looking down at us, like you know. When all the people look down at you as if though to say she's a young person and she's pregnant, she like supported us through that. She like helped us like feel better like that. I was quite pleased about that as well.
(Kirsty, mentored for over three years)

This was a very difficult time for Kirsty, as she had to cope with moving into her own flat as well as having a baby at a very young age.

Culture

Nat had a very good relationship with his mentor and she met all the criteria he felt he needed for a successful relationship. However, he had initially viewed mentoring as designed to help people just with practical skills for their move to independent living:

> That wouldn't have done anything for me … That would have been superficial for me. It would have been like seeing my social worker. Which means defence up always again. It helped that she was more available.

> For a person who is a bit down it needs to be more closer than what mentoring is designed to be for. Besides sorting out ... benefits and help it should be about helping the inside as well. The state of mind … Needs differ between young people so the mentoring thing should be flexible.
> (Nat, mentored for over one year)

Although Nat undoubtedly needed to improve his independent living skills, his main need was for emotional support, as he felt lonely and isolated in his flat. This was complicated by the fact that he was a young refugee and was confused about his relationship with his culture. Nat was matched with a peer mentor from his own cultural background and he saw that as critical to his successful development as an independent young man:

> After my day was finished the most traumatising time was coming home and falling asleep at home, because I grew up with a lot of family naturally. Having somewhere to go because she was local. I didn't know how to communicate with people of my own background. I was slowly being deculturalised – cos of the pain inside.

She showed me how to communicate with my own people. I thought of myself as a sell-out to my own people initially ... When I saw them and they are completely Europeanised and going to university and they do everything in the European way. Then I said it's OK. It is all right for me to adapt to this society and I don't have to keep to the version of what I think is [own culture]. It helped me to accept it was all right to be able to change.
(Nat)

Making it work

It is important not to underestimate the value of the time that mentors and their young people spend together talking. During these occasions, young people can be helped to reflect, problem solve and plan ahead in their lives.

Lee had a relationship with his mentor that involved doing activities that gave them time to talk. Although his mentor and he both took up a new sport together, they found that neither particularly enjoyed it so they both agreed to give it up. Talking was more important for this young person and they found better opportunities for this by having a pint at the pub, going for walks and going for a drive.

Lee valued the support his mentor gave him and recognised that he did not like making plans himself. His mentor helped him to sort out some housing problems he was having and was proactive in helping him to find work, albeit so far without success. Lee valued the accessibility he had to his mentor in that he could call him direct any time he felt he needed to. Lee felt his mentor supported him in every way he asked him to and helped him to follow up any interests he had.

Louis was a refugee who had quite a short relationship with his mentor. Despite his frustration because the relationship was cut short, he very much valued what he had got from the mentoring relationship:

We used to talk about education; things can happen; things I like, I enjoy. What else I can do. Where can I go?How do you make decisions and stuff.

There's a lot of things you cannot decide, or hard to make a decision, or you don't know what to do with the feeling. You talk to a mentor and they will give you some ideas.
(Louis)

Sarah was also a young refugee. She also valued being able to talk to her mentor and discuss things with her. She found this particularly helpful, as her mentor was a recent graduate and Sarah was planning to go to university herself:

> Because sometimes I just needed someone to listen to see whether basically I am being unreasonable or I needed help with something …

> She was there for all the emotional problems at the time. She was my sounding board. I used to bounce ideas off of her and she would tell me her opinions.

> It is not easy being a young person in the care system. You do become withdrawn. It is a side effect of living amongst strangers. You want to fade into the background basically most of the time. You would have problems at school; you would be socially inept at most times, or very aggressive or angry. So, yes, it does help let out most of the negative emotions that you would have.
> (Sarah)

Key points

- Most of the young people who were interviewed had a longer-term experience of mentoring having been mentored for more than six months (two-thirds), including a third mentored between a year and three years.

- The mentor's gender and ethnicity, as well as their experience of care and parenthood, could contribute to successful matching.

- In the context of their transition to independence and the many changes taking place in their lives, young people's initial action plans and goals were subject to many changes.

- Mentors generally worked with young people to agree their goals and carry out their action plans. It was a negotiated process rather than an imposed one.

- The longer-term mentoring relationships were generally intensive both in terms of length and frequency of meetings.

- Young people valued the accessibility, attention and informality of the mentoring relationship, contrasting this with professional help. Mentoring was also seen as different from relationships with partners or friends.

- There were differences between traditional adult one-to-one mentoring and peer mentoring. The former discouraged drawing on the mentor's own background whereas this was central to the rationale of peer mentoring.

- Most of the mentoring relationships included 'instrumental' and 'expressive' dimensions.

5 Being a mentor: the views of mentors

Being your mentor … Like being an older sister, if you mess up I will be there to help and if you do well I will be there to congratulate you.
(Mentor)

This chapter is based on interviews with 11 mentors from five projects that covered 12 mentoring relationships. All of the mentors involved in the Prince's Trust Leaving Care Initiative mentoring projects were volunteers and received payments only for expenses. We begin by presenting a profile of our mentors. We then explore why they chose to get involved in mentoring, and their experiences of the training and support they received.

Profile and range

One mentor had been involved in mentoring two of the young people in the sample. The mentors interviewed ranged in age from 18 to 48. Four of the younger-aged mentors were peer mentors.

Three of the mentors were male and eight were female, and one of the mentors mentored two of the young people interviewed in the research. Proportionately, the largest ethnic background was white British (six), with a further two mentors being white European. Three of the mentors were black, one being black African, one black Caribbean and one black British.

Five of the mentors had been educated to degree level, three to Intermediate GNVQ, two had completed their education at GCSE level and the education level attained by one mentor was not known. At the time they started mentoring, three were employed at management level, two were working in social care occupations and one was a student of social care. In total, two were students. One of the mentors was unemployed and one was a full-time parent. Their hobbies included active participation in sporting activities, cultural pursuits, home-making skills, motorcycling, socialising and travelling.

Previous experience

Five of the mentors had been in care themselves and one of these had also had previous experience of working with vulnerable young people, including other care leavers. Of the other six, all but one had some experience of working with young people, either in a voluntary or paid capacity, and some also had experience of working with vulnerable young people or young people who had been care. This included having children of their own, voluntary work with young people around education issues, youth work and teaching young offenders.

Their view of the mentoring role

Most of the mentors had a fairly good idea of what mentoring entailed, although some thought that the relationship would be more goal focused and structured than it turned out to be in practice. They soon found out that they needed to be more flexible and to appreciate the small achievements in their young people's lives:

> I went in thinking I would have an objective. We would set an objective at the beginning and I would have a year to meet this objective with this young person. And I think for a while I really believed that that was going to happen. But actually it didn't.

> On reflection, that's not such a bad thing. And there wasn't one great achievement that I felt at the end of the year that I had achieved, but there were lots of little things that we achieved together.
> (Melanie)

Peter, who mentored two of the young people, also realised that his original view of the mentor role was too goal focused:

> Helping someone improve themselves and helping someone to actually get somewhere in life. That's what my perception was but in reality it is not about that …

> Reality is, it is often just being there, just listening and being someone who says 'How are you today? Have a good day.' Just by being there you can actually make a huge difference to somebody's life. Maybe you'll never know that.

> Where you have a day where you think, which is quite often, 'I'm not
> really doing anything here', I think you are maybe making more of a
> difference than you think.
> (Peter)

One of the slightly older mentors saw herself in more of a 'granny' role. Her young
woman had young children, and she saw her role as someone who would listen to
the young person and also chat with her:

> In her situation, she had a couple of kids, so I was there in a granny role,
> a sort of listening, chatting role. A lot of stuff you do if you have a friend
> round for a cup of coffee.
> (Pauline)

From the peer-mentoring project, a couple of the mentors saw themselves more in
the role of an older sibling, and someone to offer guidance and advice from their own
experience:

> Like being an older sister was my perception of the whole thing. 'If you
> mess up I will be there to help and if you do well I will be there to
> congratulate you.'
> (Marion)

Motivation

Four of the mentors had been drawn to volunteering for this work because they felt
that they would have liked to have someone like a mentor when they were growing
up. Two of these had not been in care themselves but one felt she had a difficult time
growing up and another had not been brought up by her parents.

A number of mentors expressed the need to put something back into the community,
perhaps because they felt privileged in some way and wanted to help those who
were more disadvantaged. Peter had enjoyed working with disadvantaged young
people in a voluntary capacity in his twenties and now felt he owed a debt to society:

> I do enjoy life and I feel quite privileged so I just thought it would be nice
> to be able to put something back to people who aren't.
> (Peter)

One mentor whose children had successfully reached adulthood felt she had good parenting skills, and she wanted to use these skills to help others. She had worked in prisons in the past and strongly felt that, if some of these people had different people in their lives when they were younger, their lives would have been different:

> As a teenager, as a girl teenager, you are going to hate your mum anyway. So another mum substitute, average adult, you know, type person, is an alternative role model.
> (Pauline)

For five of the mentors, the final impetus had come from seeing an advertisement for mentors, either in the *Big Issue* or through a circular at their place of work. These mentors had been thinking of volunteering in some capacity for a while and hearing about the need for mentors encouraged them to apply.

Training

All of the mentors found the training interesting and personally valuable in terms of the knowledge gained and through practical experiences like role play. They found that the training did not tell them exactly how to mentor their young person, but it made them aware of the relevant issues and enabled them to draw on their personal resources to develop the mentoring relationship. The training built on their personal qualities but was not a substitute for them.

One of the mentors initially had particular difficulties communicating with her young person. The young person became very withdrawn and turned the volume up on the radio to prevent her mentor talking with her. She was then forced to draw on her own resources to deal with this situation:

> I remember trying everything I had been taught during the training. And I just got to the stage where I thought this isn't going to work. Nothing has worked. I have tried everything. What am I going to do now? … everything's failed!

> And I thought if you can't beat her join her, cos she was singing at the top of her voice … So I sang at the top of my voice because I didn't know what else to do. And she turned and looked at me as if I was mad. And then we both just started laughing and that was it. It broke the ice, whatever it was, it broke the ice. It built up gradually from there on in.
> (Melanie)

Also, while initially some of the mentors did not feel prepared for the task they had taken on, as the relationship developed with their young people they were able to draw on some of the elements of the training:

> Before I actually met with any young people I was incredibly nervous and I don't think I was alone in that. In terms of being very nervous about taking on the one-to-one relationship … that and the ongoing training I felt had prepared me. I didn't think it had before I met the young person, but once I got into working with them I realised it had.
> (Suzanne)

Some of the mentors felt that the training almost gave them too much information and was too intense but, as they got to know their young people, they found the training experience invaluable. Mentors found that the training in particular helped them to set boundaries with their young people, and was concerned with mentor responsibilities and issues of safety. Although, for some mentors, the training seemed very comprehensive, inevitably there were some things that came up in a relationship that had not been covered by the training.

The mentors in general felt that the training did have to be fairly general and, when difficult questions did come up in the course of the relationship, they felt able to deal with them through the support given by their co-ordinator.

Support

Most of the mentors were satisfied with the level of support they received from the project co-ordinators. Mentors received both group supervision in the company of other mentors and individual one-to-one supervision with their project co-ordinator or supervisor. The group supervision sessions were also often used as an opportunity to offer further training to mentors, often on specific topics. From the interviews with project co-ordinators as well as mentors, it is apparent that these sessions are not always very well supported because of the time constraints faced by busy mentors, who prioritised time with their young people over group work. According to the mentors, group supervision took place in the projects on a monthly to six-weekly basis.

One-to-one supervision was generally held less often, between monthly and quarterly. However, one mentor who was very dissatisfied with the levels of support she had received while mentoring said that she had not had an individual supervision session. The mentor felt that the monthly group-supervision sessions were not an appropriate place to raise some of the issues she was having with her young person. The previous project co-ordinator had long-term sick leave and this mentor felt that there had been no one there to deputise. The co-ordinator subsequently left the project and the support was reported to have improved with the appointment of the co-ordinator's successor. Another mentor from the same project also commented that she had waited a year before she had a one-to-one support meeting, but had not felt this was a problem. When she had a need for support or advice she would telephone the co-ordinator, which she felt was more convenient than arranging a formal session at the office.

The project was set within a busy city leaving care team and the co-ordinator had a number of roles within the team apart from co-ordinating the mentoring project. Two mentors from the same project had slightly different views of the success of the project co-ordinator in managing the support of the mentors when faced with the difficulties of managing the other competing needs within her job:

> I think our co-ordinator is a miracle worker. I don't know how she wears all the different hats she does and doesn't let any balls drop.
> (Suzanne)

Peter had talked to the co-ordinator about the problems he felt there were with the support and found her willing to listen to suggestions. He also appreciated that there were cost implications for the project of having a full time co-ordinator. Although he and other mentors did feel that the level of support received was adequate, they would have liked the impetus for contact to come from the project rather than the individual mentor:

> But I have often thought that social services is probably doing the mentoring thing as well as their main job. So the mentoring was not their day job … Tagged on and sometimes there isn't really any support there.
> (Peter)

A number of mentors commented that they were assured that the support was there if they needed it, as they were able to make telephone contact with the project co-ordinator. One of the project co-ordinators did make a point of telephoning mentors just prior to or after they were due to meet with their young people to check whether they had any specific support needs.

The peer mentors all said that they felt very supported by the project co-ordinator. He made himself available to them when they needed to speak to someone and was always available by mobile telephone. They saw him almost in a parental role while they were more like older siblings to their young people. The group meetings at the peer mentoring project were for both mentors and their young people and did not fulfil the same role as the group support in the other projects. These meetings were usually focused around some activity where mentors could get to know and help their young people where appropriate.

Key points

■ Mentors were well equipped for this role by some combination of personal experience, having been in care themselves, or being a parent, or their previous or current work experience with young people.

■ The mentor's own experience of growing up, being in care, being a parent, feeling privileged themselves and wanting to give something back, and responding to recruitment publicity were all cited as reasons for mentoring.

■ Training was seen as very helpful, especially during the course of a longer-term relationship. Mentors also received and valued both group supervision and one-to-one supervision with the project co-ordinator.

■ The mentor's initial perception of their role was often very goal orientated but that was likely to change over time as they recognised the complexity and subtlety of the process. Small changes and 'just being there' for someone could be valued by young people.

6 Making a difference? The views of young people and their mentors

Looking back, did mentoring make a difference to you?

When I got older I started to realise how they helped me, but I didn't see it at the time.

This chapter discusses the outcomes of mentoring relationships as seen by both the young people and their mentors. The young people were asked about key areas of their lives that they worked on with their mentors and if in their view that intervention made any difference to them. Finally, we consider the impact of mentoring on the mentors.

Outcomes – making a difference

Mentors were not involved to a large extent in matters relating to young people's accommodation. This was usually dealt with by other agencies. However, young people did appreciate their mentor's advice on decorating their accommodation and buying furniture cheaply. They also received help and advice with independent living skills, budgeting and completing forms relating to accommodation and benefits. One mentor and young person spent time at the local library finding out about things someone who has moved to independence may need to know. This was then collated into a folder that the young person found invaluable in managing her flat.

Most of the mentors talked about education, training or employment with their young people. Many of the mentors were active in helping the young people find work and also gave help and support to them with writing their curricula vitae and helping them look for work on the internet. One young man was particularly pleased, as his mentor had contacts within the industry he wished to enter and put him in touch with them. Another young man commented that, although his mentor was giving advice and support, the young man was not ready to listen initially. But eventually he did take notice of his mentor when she gave him an ultimatum to stay unemployed or do something with his life.

Young people commented that their mentors had helped improve their confidence. One young woman with a mental health problem found that her mentor was particularly helpful in addressing some of the disadvantages of this condition:

> She explained the different people and how they react and how they communicate and then gave me goals, like, go and chat to somebody and things like that. Very scary but I managed it …

> She taught me how to communicate and, if I don't understand something, to ask, and explained a lot about how to build your self-esteem up.
> (Danielle)

Sometimes mentors were able to introduce their young people to other groups of young people that helped them to build up their confidence. Within the peer-mentoring scheme, one mentor introduced her young person to her own family and friends who helped him to expand his own social networks. Many of the young people and mentors from the project were involved in group work there, which again helped them to develop their own social networks. In the other projects, it was not considered appropriate for young people to be introduced to people in the mentor's life and in particular family members.

Many of the mentors were involved in discussing relationships and how to manage them with the young people. One mentor supported her young person when she was going through a period of domestic violence and marriage break-up. The young person felt able to discuss the situation with her mentor and mentioned that, had she not had a mentor, she would just have kept quiet about her problems and difficulties. Another mentor acted as an advocate between her young person and her mother, which was very much appreciated by the young person as it healed the rift between them.

Young people reported that they had achieved in a number of areas, which they credited to the mentoring relationship. These included independent living skills, social skills, stability, confidence and self-esteem.

Where they found their mentors help most valuable was generally in terms of building their self-confidence, improving their emotional well-being and developing their social and practical skills. Although this was perhaps difficult to measure, the young people interviewed were sure that it was their mentoring relationship that had helped them in these areas:

> She has helped me bring my confidence up so I can trust myself and doing things more, and believe in things I never used to.

Although the young people we interviewed generally had successful mentoring relationships, they did recognise that mentoring had its limitations. Mentors could not necessarily help them in all areas of their lives, nor would they expect them to. However, they did find it difficult to identify specific areas where their mentor was unable to help them.

But not all of the young people were satisfied with their mentoring relationship. Louis had a mentor who he felt was too busy to see him. Although he felt there were some benefits of the relationship in terms of building his confidence through the mentor's encouragement, he felt that other areas where he needed help were not satisfactorily completed:

> If we had enough time maybe we could have succeeded or maybe we finish our aim or something. At that time you know in a way it was quite helpful. It been nice but there was no conclusion. It was something you start but never finish.
> (Louis)

Did mentors think they made a difference?

Mentors and their young people were in some agreement about the outcomes of their mentoring relationships.

Tracey was a young single parent when she started being mentored. She had learning difficulties and was also agoraphobic. By the end of the relationship, she was able to use public transport and had joined some groups at her local community centre. Her mentor, Suzanne, felt she had made an impact on Tracey, by giving her support to overcome her fear step by step. Suzanne and Tracey both commented that her self-esteem and confidence had improved and that she was now able to look after both herself and her flat better than previously. While Tracey felt mentoring had made a significant impact on her, Suzanne was less confident:

> I still had the constant bugbear of agreeing a target for the next session and she never did the target.
> (Suzanne)

Clarice commented that her mentor helped her to be more positive in her outlook on life, and her mentor Jackie felt that mentoring had made a difference to Clarice's self-esteem and confidence. Although the relationship has officially ended, Clarice does still contact Jackie if she needs help:

> It has helped her … just to guide her really … Before she didn't do much
> with herself … she didn't have loads of self-esteem but now she has
> picked herself up and she is trying to do things for herself now.
> (Jackie)

Jez and Jenny, his mentor, both commented on how the relationship had improved
Jez's self-esteem and confidence. Jenny felt that having a female mentor had been
of benefit to Jez, as he did not have many female friends. She felt that having an
older person who could advise him in a non-professional capacity was an important
benefit for him and also made him feel more valued.

Whereas Vanessa was getting professional advice on parenting, it was only when
her mentor, Pauline, reinforced this advice that Vanessa began to put it into practice.
However, Pauline also felt that changes in Vanessa's social and practical skills and
confidence were due equally to increasing maturity as she approached her mid-
twenties. Vanessa acknowledged that there had been a lot of changes in her life but
did feel that her mentor was a real help to her, as she trusted her more than other
people who were involved in her life. Pauline felt that they had a good relationship
that meant that the young person felt at ease to speak freely to her about anything.

Jake felt that he was not able to get to know his young man very well partly because
of differences in their personality and also because he left the project after only six
months. This hampered what they were able to achieve. Paul, similarly, felt that the
relationship had been too short to make much of an impact on his life:

> I wasn't a guy, sort of jack the lad … I wasn't the coolest guy … I was
> more sensible. Kind of like an older brother. You know sometimes an
> older or younger brother, kind of, sort of, don't look up to one another.
> The younger one sort of wants to go a slightly different way. I think that's
> how me and Paul were together. Perhaps that's why we never got to
> bond together really well.
> (Jake)

Hayley's mentor offered her support while she was at college and felt that this did
have a positive effect. He also thought mentoring had made a difference in terms of
her communication with her social worker. He also supported her in how she dealt
with her pregnancy. But, despite this, he was still unsure whether he had made a
difference to her life.

Peter gave his young person, Lee, a large amount of advice and support to help him find employment and training. However, although Lee had been on some short courses, he had been unable to secure employment. Peter and Lee had a very good relationship and were friends. Although Lee had the same issues he had when they met, Peter felt that he was a bit happier and that his practical and social skills, as well as his confidence, had improved because of the relationship. Lee also felt that these areas in his life had improved and valued his mentor's support, as he felt that without a mentor he would have done nothing.

Emma helped Kirsty with her social skills so that she felt more confident communicating with people and making her own decisions. She felt that sometimes she was the only one to accept the young person for who she was. Kirsty was reluctant to discuss parenting problems with social workers for fear of being labelled as a bad parent. Emma felt she had made a difference to Kirsty in terms of how Kirsty now saw herself, which was backed up by the project co-ordinator who had seen changes in the young person, and the young person herself. The mentor felt that having a shared care experience helped in the relationship.

Elizabeth felt that her relationship with Danielle was too short to have made any impact on her except possibly in terms of self-esteem. However, Danielle did feel that mentoring helped. She felt that it built up her confidence and helped her in terms of her relationships and being able to ask for support if she needed it. This was important to Danielle as her mental health problems compromised her ability to communicate.

Marion credited the mentoring scheme with making a difference to her young person, Danny. She felt that it was the group work carried on at the project rather than the one-to-one mentoring relationship that was the key benefit to him. The mentoring relationship had been very short, as Marion had moved to a different area and she also commented that the gap between her achievements and her mentee were too big for him to relate to. A positive aspect of the relationship was that Danny got to know her friends and did not feel that he had to impress them in the same way as his own mates. Danny did feel that Marion had been a great help to him in pointing out the realities of independent living and in guiding him:

> She point me in the right direction. If she didn't point me in the right
> direction I wouldn't be here today like as I am now.
> (Danny)

Melanie felt that reliability was an important part of the support she gave her young person, Claire:

> I used to get quite a lot out of it. I used to look forward to seeing her. I never let her down. It was important that, I felt it was important that she knew I would be there. Whilst all these things were a bit unstable in her life I felt it was important that she knew she could rely on me.
> (Melanie)

The mentoring relationship offered Claire some stability when she was going through big changes in her life. Melanie and Claire were friends but also had a positive working relationship according to the mentor:

> Someone that wasn't involved or being paid. Part of a team that was supporting her but someone from outside that was doing it because they wanted to.
> (Melanie)

Longer-term impact

Young people found it quite difficult to identify the long-term impacts of having a mentor. So many things had changed in their lives during this transitional period that it was difficult for them to be able to say that it was their mentor that made all the difference in their lives. Some of the young people felt that, while they were being mentored, they were not sure of the value of the service but, since that time, they have come to realise how much they have benefited.

John, who was involved in substance abuse and offending in the past, had two mentors in total. He was now looking forward to a future in the services and on reflection sees the value of his mentoring relationships:

> Not at that time but when I got older I started to realise how they helped me, which was better for me. But I didn't see it at that time. They did actually learn me more stuff than I imagined. Not at that time cos I was too young. I wanted to go out with my mates and that. I saw him a couple of weeks back and I told him thanks for trying to help me.

> That's what he was trying to do. Yeah, they have made a difference. Because actually now I have been out of trouble. I haven't done one thing wrong for five years, which is good for me. They made a big difference. They were helping me out. I ended up seeing why they were always having a go at me. Eventually!
> (John)

One young woman had felt at the time she was being mentored that it was making a slight difference to her but since then had begun to realise how big the impact was once the relationship had come to an end:

> It wasn't a big impact until I stopped seeing her. Then it became like
> WOW!
> (Danielle)

Her mentoring relationship had lasted for a year and the ending had been planned. She felt she was more outgoing, more chatty and could communicate easily. She also commented that she had learned to read and respond to the body language of others and was more aware of her own. This was particularly important to her as she had a mental health problem that made these things difficult for her. All of this led to an improvement in her self-esteem. Although other professionals were involved in her life, she identified the mentor as being the one that helped with this.

Looking back, looking forward

All of the young people interviewed did have some plans for their future. One young person felt that she could not really make plans and was only able to take one day at a time, but she was able to look forwards in that she wanted to improve her numeracy skills and move to be nearer to her family. She also had career aspirations.

Only two of the young people were totally focused around domesticity. One of them had experienced parenting difficulties in the past but was now looking forward to building her life with her daughter and partner:

> My plans for the future are giving my daughter the best in life. Being with
> my partner till death do us part and getting married.
> (Vanessa)

Having a job was important to most of the young people in terms of their future, and eight of the young people had clear aspirations to improve their education and pursue a career. For three of them this meant running their own businesses. Three of the young people also felt it was important for them to do some voluntary work helping others as they had been helped in the past:

I would like to think life is beautiful. Which means I need to be successful so I would like to have a business of my own. And if not I would like to have steady employment. Being someone who is helping a lot of other people as I can see myself as helping other people as well as primarily helping myself.
(Nat)

I have to do voluntary work I have to give back what I spent the last six years studying or learning or living or experiencing. To give back some of that.
(Nat)

Improving the mentoring experience

Careful matching and a flexible approach emerged as key areas young people would like to see improved:

By being more flexible and personal for the person's needs, by being experience orientated rather than regulated – you do this once a week or anything like that. By spending more time with the young person and not just assigning them the next available mentor.
(Nat)

Flexibility was also emphasised by another young man, Jez. He felt that the time restriction placed on mentoring meetings by the project hampered the work that could be done effectively when they met. For example, library visits could take more than the allocated hour, which resulted in the mentor leaving before they had completed the activities they had planned for the session.

One young woman commented that the budgetary constraints of the project should not prevent mentors and their young people meeting frequently if that was what the young person needed. She felt that she needed to see her mentor at least once a week and sometimes more but there was insufficient funding to pay for travel more often than once a month. She lived quite far from her mentor. The problem would not have arisen if they had lived near each other.

Two of the young people commented that they felt they would have got more from the relationship if they had an action plan and one mentioned the benefit of having regular meeting times. However, this was not the case for all of the young people who did not have a formal plan.

One young woman strongly felt that a mentor during the time of transition represented some continuity in her life. For her, it was important that this person would be able to stay around in her life for as long as she needed her to mitigate some of the instability and constant change created by the 'looked after' system:

> When you are in care you go through foster homes, you go through children's homes, you go through a whole list of different social workers. You need someone there who's going to be there. You know.
>
> Cos when you leave care, you're in a flat, you're by yourself, you know. You need someone there to support you. Not everyone has family, not everyone has friends, but I think a mentor is essential.
> (Clarice – mentored for over three years)

Conversely, one young woman who was involved in a project that limited the length of mentoring relationships was now on her third mentoring relationship. She would have preferred to stay with the same mentor for as long as she needed her support rather than having to change to a new mentor every year.

The impact on mentors

Young people were not the only people who the mentoring relationship had an impact on. Many of the mentors found that the experience had a profound effect on their lives and attitudes. For some this even meant a career change.

Attitudes, self-esteem and confidence

All of the mentors found the process of mentoring together with the training an empowering experience, and most found that their self-esteem and self-confidence were improved through doing it:

> It has been rewarding for us, even when there's been problems and things. You can see what you are getting out of it. You know.
> (Emma)

The impact of mentoring touched the lives of most of the mentors in such a way that they had changed or were thinking of changing their careers in order to work with young people. Although Suzanne had already been considering a career change, the effect of mentoring helped her to crystallize her thoughts and make the change. Mentoring helped her better understand the complex needs of the young people and challenged her original view of mentoring that it would enable all the young people's needs to be met:

> I think the impact for me was huge in terms of both the reality of understanding just how complex some of these young people's needs are … and the need to recognise the small successes.
>
> I think maybe when all of us in the training, when we started mentoring, were expecting that we would leave our young people totally sorted and up together, and, you know, in no need of any help or assistance, and I found that was not realistic unless you wanted to mentor them for most of the rest of their life.
> (Suzanne)

Another mentor felt that now, after mentoring two young people, he was a better mentor. He had learned not to expect major changes in young people's lives but to accept that mentoring may facilitate a more measured period of change:

> I learnt from there that you might just do a little bit and it might help a lot. Not to expect big jumps and things might move very slowly.

His mentoring experience had also led him to consider a career change in the future and, in the meantime, he had become more involved in mentoring, undertaking further training as part of his job.

Three of the mentors were studying social work at the time of their interviews and two others had gained mentoring qualifications. One mentor had built on her mentoring experience by taking a certificate in teaching basic skills, as she felt this would be helpful in her mentoring relationship. She was also considering a career change to social work or a similar occupation.

Skills gained through mentoring

All of the mentors felt that they had gained or improved skills through the training and mentoring experience. Skills they mentioned in particular were listening skills, and gaining a better understanding of young people and the difficulties they face. They also talked about becoming more aware of the wider society and where young people fitted into that:

> ... that makes you think ... Because it is wrong ... All the things that ... you become very aware that there is this strata of society that are judged and that are doing exactly what we do ... And yet what they do is perceived in a totally different way.
> (Pauline)

All of the peer mentors interviewed felt that they were now better able to relate to other young people and two of them were going on to do other work with young people as their career. They felt they had gained communication skills, relationship skills and a better understanding of commitment:

> It is good to help somebody. Makes you feel a bit better. Seeing other people getting to their goals and just help them really.
> (Jackie, peer mentor)

What could be improved?

When asked to reflect on their experience of mentoring, project support was mentioned as a key part of the process. Where projects had staff changes resulting in support being intermittent or missing, this was seen as inherently problematic. Mentors felt that their support should be prioritised, as often they did not feel totally confident in dealing with everything that they needed to deal with in the course of their mentoring relationship.

A number of mentors mentioned that it would have been helpful to meet some of the young people on their training programme, as to some extent they could not envisage the difficulties faced by care leavers and what sort of support they would be looking for from their mentors. Some also felt they did not really know what to expect, and what the young people expected, of the mentoring process.

Key points

- The young people we interviewed thought that mentoring helped them with important practical advice, particularly in relation to maintaining their accommodation, discussing education, employment and training, and finding work.

■ Mentoring was also highly valued by young people for helping them with relationship problems, building their confidence and improving their emotional well-being.

■ The mentor's views of the impact of mentoring generally reflected the young people's views.

■ The longer-term impact of mentoring as seen by young people is difficult to measure, given the many influences on their lives. However, some of the young people felt on reflection that mentoring had been helpful to them even though they may have not recognised its value at the time.

■ The mentoring experience had a significant impact on the mentors. All of them thought they had improved their skills and confidence in helping young people and, as a consequence, most wanted to work with young people.

■ For young people, mentoring could be improved by better matching, greater flexibility and less time restrictions on meeting and the length of mentoring relationships.

■ For mentors, more consistent and accessible support, and involving young people in their training, would improve mentoring.

7 Conclusion

Research summary

This study set out to explore the longer-term mentoring experiences and outcomes of young people leaving care. Information was collected through a file search and interviews with young people and their mentors on ongoing mentoring relationships that lasted between six months and three years, as well as mentoring relationships that had ended between two and four years earlier. In addition, policy interviews were carried out with project leaders.

In exploring this area we began by describing the mentoring projects. The projects in our study were set up under the Prince's Trust Leaving Care Initiative and were developed in response to the vulnerability of young people leaving care during their journey to adulthood: isolation, lack of support, possible mental health problems and the need for additional services at the time of transition were all cited as reasons. Our projects were funded by the Prince's Trust for the recruitment, training and supervision of mentors (all projects) and by different partnership arrangements between local authorities and voluntary organisations. Most of the projects were either based in specialist leaving care teams or had developed links with them. Most of the projects had well-developed systems for mentor selection, training, support, matching and feedback.

The main type of mentoring provided by the projects was volunteer and one-to-one mentoring. This has included two approaches. First, 'traditional' adult mentoring that aimed to compensate vulnerable young people for the absence of a consistent and caring adult to give guidance, and, historically, influenced by Rutter's research on resilience (Rutter, 1987). Second, peer mentoring, derived from recognition of the contribution to be made by care leavers who have 'been there' themselves, in mentoring those embarking on a similar journey.

Mentoring relationships were likely to include both 'instrumental' task-focused and 'expressive' befriending roles, although there were differences in emphasis between projects and there was no uniform development from one of these dimensions to the other.

Problematic areas identified by project leaders included the impact of defined time limits on young people; boundaries within mentoring relationships – these varied across the projects; and possible confusion between mentors and personal advisers appointed under the Children (Leaving Care) Act 2000.

We then presented the findings from the analysis of our database. This provided us with data on 181 mentoring relationships from 13 projects. Most young people were matched with a mentor within two months and they were referred, or referred themselves, for a wide variety of reasons. Wanting a 'listener' or 'role model', help with 'independent living skills', exploring their 'options and plans' and 'general support' were the most cited reasons. Mentors worked with young people on both 'instrumental' and 'expressive' areas. The former included education, employment and training, and practical skills, and the latter confidence and self-esteem.

As regards outcomes, three-quarters of young people 'achieved their goals' and over half had achieved other goals that emerged during the mentoring relationship. Most young people (93 per cent) had some 'positive outcome' by the end of the mentoring relationship. This included either an 'instrumental' goal achievement or a more 'expressive' dimension, such as improving their confidence or ability to sustain relationships. Negative outcomes included lack of engagement, missing appointments and unplanned endings – often linked to their chaotic lives. A significant number of unplanned endings were due to the mentor withdrawing and this caused distress to some young people. However, where young people had unplanned endings, some also had achieved positive outcomes prior to that time.

Young people who were mentored for over a year were more likely to have achieved their original goals and to have future plans. Also, the longer the mentoring relationship lasted, the more likelihood there was of a positive outcome. Nearly two-fifths (39 per cent) of the young people had made some plans for their future in at least one area of their lives by the end of the mentoring relationship.

Our interviews with 17 young people complemented this picture. Most of the young people who were interviewed had a longer-term experience of mentoring, having been mentored for more than six months (two-thirds), including a third mentored between a year and three years.

We found that young people felt it was important they were matched with a mentor who they could trust and get on with, and that the mentor's gender and ethnicity as well as their experience of care (peer mentors) and parenthood could contribute to successful matching, although the skill of the mentor may mitigate initial apprehension that the young people had about the matching. Also, longer-term mentoring relationships were generally intensive in terms of both the length and frequency of meetings.

In the context of their transition to independence and the many changes taking place in their lives, young people's initial action plans and goals were subject to many changes. Mentors generally worked with young people to agree their goals and carry out their action plans. It was thus a negotiated process rather than an imposed one. Most of these longer-term mentoring relationships included both 'instrumental' and 'expressive' dimensions. Young people valued the accessibility, attention and informality of the mentoring relationship, contrasting this with professional help. Mentoring was also seen as different from relationships with partners or friends.

Our interviews with mentors revealed that they viewed their motivation for their mentoring role as being derived from some combination of personal experience – their own difficulties in growing up, or having been in care themselves, or being a parent – and their previous or current work experience with young people. 'Putting something back' mattered to them.

Their initial perception of their role was often very 'instrumental' or goal orientated but that was likely to change over time. As their relationship developed with young people, they recognised the complexity and subtlety of the process; small changes and just 'being there' were often valued by young people. Training was seen as very helpful, especially during the course of a longer-term relationship. Mentors also received both group supervision and one-to-one supervision with the project co-ordinator.

Finally, we looked at the longer-term impact on the young people of their mentoring relationships. Most of the young people we interviewed valued the advice they received from the mentors during their transition to independence. They thought that mentoring helped them with important practical advice, particularly in relation to maintaining their accommodation, discussing education, employment and training, and finding work.

Mentoring was also highly valued by young people for helping them with relationship problems, building their confidence and improving their emotional well-being. The mentor's views of the impact of mentoring generally reflected the young people's views.

The longer-term impact of mentoring as seen by young people is difficult to measure, given the many influences on their lives. However, some of the young people felt on reflection that mentoring had been helpful to them even though they may not have recognised its value at the time.

The mentoring experience also had a significant impact on the mentors. All of them thought they had improved their skills and confidence in helping young people and, as a consequence, most wanted to work with young people.

We also asked both young people and mentors how mentoring could be improved. Our young people thought that better matching, greater flexibility and less time restrictions on meeting and the length of mentoring relationships would help. For mentors, more consistent and accessible support, and involving young people in their training, would improve mentoring.

Mentoring and leaving care policy and practice

A consistent finding from studies of care leavers is that a majority move to independent living at just 16 or 17, whereas most of their peers remain at home well into their twenties, and, for many of these young people, leaving care is a final event, there is no option to return in times of difficulty. Also, they often have to cope with major status changes in their lives at the time of leaving care: leaving foster care or their children's home and setting up a new home, and for some young people starting a family as well; leaving school and finding their way into further education, training or employment, or coping with unemployment. These studies have also shown the high risk of social exclusion of care leavers (Stein, 2004).

Against this background, the law has been strengthened by the introduction of the Children (Leaving Care) Act 2000. The role of the personal adviser is central to the implementation of the Act's main provisions including needs assessment and pathway planning. Why then, paradoxically, given the enhanced contribution of professional support, including more structured assessment and planning processes, is there a role for volunteer mentors, as this study suggests?

Mentoring – a different kind of relationship?

The answer is, in part, that volunteer adult and peer mentoring is seen by these young people to offer a different type of relationship from professional help and also, for some, from their troubled family relationships. The mentor cited in Chapter 6, who despaired when she couldn't engage her young person, despite trying out all she had been taught in training, captures the essence of mentoring:

> I thought if you can't beat her join her, cos she was singing at the top of her voice ... So I sang at the top of my voice because I didn't know what else to do. And she turned and looked at me as if I was mad. And then we both just started laughing and that was it. It broke the ice, whatever it was, it broke the ice. It built up gradually from there on in.

The two models outlined at the beginning of our report suggested that mentoring could first be identified by *purpose*, on an 'instrumental' to 'expressive' continuum, and second by *process*, on a 'service-led' to 'participatory' continuum.

Our study suggests that successful mentoring for young people leaving care usually combines 'instrumental' and 'expressive' dimensions during the course of the relationship. One dimension may lead to the other, but in any direction. Young people were allowed to go both forwards and backwards, more akin to normative transitions, but, ironically, this is often denied care leavers, who are expected to follow a clear pathway to independence.

Also, what was seen by young people and their mentors as shaping the development of the relationship was the *process.* The balance between instrumental and expressive dimensions depended mainly on the responsiveness of the mentor to the changing needs and circumstances of the young person. Goal setting was part of this dynamic process – set goals were often changed and new ones agreed, linked to the young person's changing life course. It was at best a flexible and negotiated process, working with, not on, young people. There was no evidence to support a simple instrumental or progression model of mentoring.

For young people leaving care who are coping with challenges of significant transitions, mentoring may provide a different kind of additional support – and that may in part explain why mentoring has been identified in the international literature as promoting the resilience of young people from disadvantaged backgrounds (Stein, 2004). A greater recognition of the contribution of mentoring may lead to the wider availability of mentoring projects, working alongside personal advisers, in assisting young people leaving care.

In conclusion, in the context of an increasingly formalised, professional and target-driven culture in education, child welfare and youth policy, mentoring is able to offer a complementary but different experience of a relationship to young people at the critical period of their transition to adulthood, young people who also often lack consistent support by their families. Or, as one young person put it, 'having someone for me'.

References

Cathcart J. (ed.) (2003) *Mentoring – Leaving Care Initiative, Toolkit Issue 2*. London: The Prince's Trust

Clayden, J. and Stein, M. (2002) *Mentoring for Care Leavers*. London: The Prince's Trust

Colley, H. (2003) *Mentoring for Social Inclusion: A Critical Approach to Nurturing Mentor Relationships*. London: Routledge Farmer

Department of Health (DoH) (1998) *Quality Protects: Framework for Action*. London: DoH

Department of Health (1999) *Me, Survive, Out There? New Arrangements for Young People Living in and Leaving Care*. London: DoH

Department of Health (2001) *Children (Leaving Care) Act 2000; Regulations and Guidance*. London: DoH

DuBois, D.L., Holloway, B.E., Valentine, J.C. and Cooper, H. (2002) 'Effectiveness of mentoring programs for youth: a meta-analytical review', *American Journal of Community Psychology*, Vol. 30, No. 2, pp. 157–97

Philip, K., King, C. and Shucksmith, J. (2004) *Sharing a Laugh? A Qualitative Study of Mentoring Interventions with Young People*. York: JRF

Rutter, M. (1987) 'Psychosocial resilience and protective mechanisms', *American Journal of Orthopsychiatry*, Vol. 57, pp. 316–31

Sherman, L.W., Gottfredson, D., MacKenzie, D., Eck, J., Reuter, P. and Bushway, S. (1997) *Preventing Crime: What Works, What Doesn't, What's Promising*. Maryland, MD: Department of Criminology and Criminal Justice, University of Maryland. http://www.ncjrs.org/works

Shiner, M., Young, T., Newburn, T. and Groben, S. (2004) *Mentoring Disaffected Young People: An Evaluation of Mentoring Plus*. York: JRF

Shiner, M., Young, T., Newburn, T. and Groben, S. (2004) 'Mentoring Disaffected Young People: An Evaluation of Mentoring Plus', *Findings*, No. 644, p. 2. York: JRF

Social Exclusion Unit (1998a) *Rough Sleeping.* London: TSO

Social Exclusion Unit (1998b) *Truancy and Social Exclusion.* London: TSO

Social Exclusion Unit (1999) *Teenage Pregnancy.* London: TSO

Stein, M. (2004) *What Works for Young People Leaving Care?* Ilford: Barnardo's

Utting, W. (1997) *People Like Us: Report of the Review of the Safeguards for Children Living Away from Home.* London: TSO

Appendix: Detailed description of the projects involved in the research

This Appendix provides a brief profile of the projects involved in the research.

Borough 1 was initially set up by a consultant and was managed by a part-time co-ordinator with some administrative assistance. It was set up to meet the Prince's Trust model of one-to-one mentoring with training meeting Prince's Trust standards but not externally accredited. The project was situated within, and managed by, a voluntary organisation that provides aftercare and housing for young people leaving care. The co-ordinator was also involved with other projects. Mentoring relationships were intended to be task-focused with action plans drawn up between the young person and their mentor at the beginning of a relationship, although this was not always the case where this was not considered appropriate.

Latterly, the project is no longer functioning as a mentoring project for care leavers because of withdrawal of funding for that part of its work as the local authority have identified other funding priorities.

Borough 2 was managed by a large voluntary organisation working with young people who are at risk of offending as well as working with care leavers. This project also offered short-term, task-centred mentoring as well as befriending. Its aim was to promote, safeguard and enhance the rights of children and young people in order to assist them to make a successful transition to adulthood and empower them to be heard. Relationships were expected to last between six and 12 months, and were reviewed on a six-monthly basis, although, for short-term, task-orientated relationships, only three to four meetings were planned. The co-ordinator was also involved in other projects as part of his role. (This is the same for Borough 1.)

Borough 3 was originally set up by another large voluntary organisation as a response to a perceived gap in provision for young people leaving care. It was physically situated in the same building as the local social services department and consequently had very strong links with the leaving care team. There was no 'drop-in' at the project but young people were very involved with the project through a user participation group, awaydays, celebration events, workshops and trips. A relatively large proportion of the young people using the project were asylum seekers. The project adopted the Prince's Trust model of one-to-one mentoring and training, and mentors chose not to have the training accredited.

Young people in mentoring relationships were encouraged to set goals and work together with a mentor to achieve those goals. The mentor was to use their skills and knowledge to help and advise the young person in order to achieve the goals. The project was oversubscribed with waiting lists for both mentor training and mentees waiting to be matched with trained mentors. The project had a high profile in the borough and also engaged in outreach work with young people.

Borough 4 offered a mentoring service to young people aged 12–21, although only a part of this service was funded by the Prince's Trust. The project was set up in order to give young people leaving care more support than the aftercare team could offer. The mentoring scheme was targeted at establishing voluntary one-to-one relationships between volunteers from the community and young people from the care system, with the aim of helping these young people develop their individual skills, knowledge and abilities to successfully make the transition from care to independent living, and generally to assist young people in their growth as individuals. Relationships were expected to last a minimum of six months and were open-ended. The project was staffed by a full-time co-ordinator and managed and situated within social services.

City 1 was a large project but the project co-ordinator was employed only part time on the project. It was set up after the Prince's Trust approached the social services department at a time when the aftercare service was expanding. It was felt that this provided a good opportunity to give extra support to care leavers. When the project was set up, it was heavily involved with a voluntary organisation, which assisted with the setting up of the mentor training.

The project was physically situated in the same building as the leaving care team and so communication between the two was very good. The project offered a:

> … structured mentoring and educational programme designed to help young people set goals for their future and reach those goals with the support of a caring volunteer mentor.

The aim was to support young people through the transition to independence and, apart from mentoring, the project also arranged group events for mentors and mentees, and was involved in many Prince's Trust events.

City 2, run by a voluntary organisation, was set up with a 'drop-in' centre for young people in care and care leavers as well as a one-to-one befriending service. This was in response to research that found that young care leavers identified feelings of isolation and a lack of support. Its purpose was to provide a place where young people could meet with others to reduce isolation. Relationships often started with volunteers through the 'drop-in' service and this developed into one-to-one mentoring relationships. There was also a peer-mentoring stream to the service.

The project did not concentrate on task-focused work with action planning, as there was recognition that at this stage in their lives young people may need just some company and the relationship to build up slowly. During this process, the mentor was then able to encourage young people to access other services. This project has moved to a more goal-oriented approach as it has developed, citing government priorities as the impetus for this.

While there was a full time co-ordinator, the project was subject to staffing changes partly because of its insecure funding situation.

City 3 was situated with and managed by a mental health voluntary organisation. The project was set up at a time when the social services department became aware that it needed to increase its services for care leavers. At the same time, a local voluntary organisation recognised that care leavers had a high incidence of mental health issues and it approached social services in order to get involved in supporting these young people. Young people using the project were encouraged to be involved with other activities at the project.

Initially, mentoring relationships were intended to be task focused, however, there was a growing realisation that befriending also played a valuable role in supporting care leavers. The project restricts mentoring relationships to one year, although young people could be rematched with a new mentor if they still needed mentoring support.

City 4 was originally based with a youth offending team and was part of a larger project that also trained and provided mentors for young offenders. The project had a dedicated project co-ordinator as well as a manager responsible for managing the other projects. The project was set up as a partnership between a voluntary organisation and the local authority.

The project's goal is to:

> ... reduce loneliness and anxiety, develop skills and confidence and help young people fulfil their potential.

It aims to recruit and train members of the local community to befriend and provide ongoing assistance to vulnerable young people who have moved to independence from the 'looked after' system. The project is an additional service for young people and is designed to complement the existing services being offered by the leaving care service. It is intended that volunteer mentoring does not replace the existing service provision but provides additional emotional and practical support for vulnerable young people.

Initially, the focus was on befriending relationships, but, during the research period, the emphasis moved towards more goal-focused mentoring relationships. The project did support some peer-mentoring relationships, although this was fairly incidental. There are currently closer links with aftercare, as the co-ordinator is based with the team.

City 5 was set up as a dedicated peer-mentoring project, to get older, successful care leavers to support younger care leavers in their transition to independence. Where a young person has a particular need for an older mentor, they can be referred to a mentoring service run by another agency. The project is based within a social services leaving care team. It works with a relatively high proportion of young people who are asylum seekers and there is a focus on group work within it. Peer mentors are trained from the age of 17, although there is no guarantee that they will become a mentor.

Mentors and mentees have a large input in the shaping of the project. They draw up boundaries and decide whether any of their peers should be excluded for inappropriate behaviour. Mentors and mentees choose when and where to meet, which is often in each other's houses, and what activities they will share.

County 1 originally had a befriending focus, with mentors offering guidance and support, developing or sharing a hobby or interest and supporting young people to develop confidence and self-esteem as well as helping them to develop their own support networks in the local community. While located within the leaving care team and funded by the local authority, it was managed by a voluntary organisation. The project had some staffing difficulties during the course of the research, but, by the second interview, the co-ordinator was in a secure full-time post.

The project was set up after research had been carried out on the leaving care team and a need had been identified for more support to be offered to care leavers. It was established in partnership with the social services department and a voluntary organisation.